CLASSIC WALKS IN

FRANCE

Rob Hunter & David Wickers

The Oxford Illustrated Press

Other books on France by Rob Hunter
include:

Walking in France
Cycle Touring in France
The Road to Compostela

– and as Neil Lands:

The Dordogne
Beyond the Dordogne
Burgundy
Brittany
The French Pyrénées
Languedoc-Roussillon

Other books by David Wickers:
Britain at Your Feet

© Text, Rob Hunter & David Wickers
1985.
© Photographs, Rob Hunter & David
Wickers 1985.
Printed in England by J. H. Haynes & Co.
Limited.
The Oxford Illustrated Press, Sparkford,
Yeovil, Somerset.
ISBN 0 946609 02 0
Distributed in America by Interbook Inc.,
14895 E 14th St., Suite 370, San Leandro,
CA 94577, USA.

All photographs supplied by the authors with the
exception of the following that were supplied by the
French Government Tourist Office:
Page 12, 42, 50, 51, 55 top, 60 top, 71, 75, 90, 91, 95,
108, 112, 121 top, 124 bottom

CONTENTS

HOW TO USE THIS BOOK

Books are written to be read, not carried about, and few walkers would think of heading off to France with this one in their rucksacks. Why take a book which covers twenty walks when only walking one of them? This is a source book, a beginning of the trip, a means to an end, and the end of it all is pleasure.

The book is divided into three main parts. The first part covers the basic elements of walking and outdoor living, and would apply anywhere, although there is a bias towards those matters and problems which are more likely to crop up in France.

The second part covers the state of walking in France itself, and lists those facilities and services which assist the walker either in the United Kingdom or within the Republic of France. As the reader will quickly realise, these facilities are widespread, more than adequate, and constantly expanding. From the sources given in this section the reader will be able to obtain large amounts of up-to-date, relevant information with which to plan his or her chosen walk.

The final, and major part of the book is the section on Classic Walks and, here again, this is divided into three sections, a basic listing of essential or advisable information sources, an outline description of the route, and the photographs. With this it should be possible for the reader to select a walk or walks which suit the length and style he or she prefers. We have tended to list *sources* rather than give specific information, for information tends to date. It takes years to research, write and publish a book, and as Josh Billings wisely remarked, 'It's better to know nothing than know what ain't so'. The basic source book for each walk is the *Topo-Guide* published by the Fédération Française de la Randonnée Pédestre, hereinafter known as the FFRP, and having selected a walk from this book, you need to buy the relevant FFRP *Topo-Guide*.

It should be said again that the choice of walks is both personal and arbitrary. We sat down with our maps and memories and tried to remember the walks we had enjoyed most, or now remember best. That gave us the bulk of the walks listed here, and friends provided the rest, urging their personal preferences as well worth a look, or reminding us, quite rightly, that different people like different things. The choice remains ours, and yours might well be different yet again.

To get the best out of this book, and pleasure from the routes it contains, you must read it to discover those walks which seem most suited to your style. We hope that our readers will follow the advice it contains, and eventually try all the walks, finding them as we have, the perfect way into the heart and heartlands of France.

GENESIS

Some years ago I completed a book called *Walking in France,* the distillation of twenty years wandering on foot through that delightful country, and designed as a comprehensive work of reference to all that France can offer to the walker.

That task done, and the book duly published, there remained a snag. A book cannot at the one time be both comprehensive and selective, a work of reference and eulogy. Yet it appeared, even as *Walking in France* was being written, that some walks outclassed the rest and deserved special consideration. Looking back over the last quarter-century, some walks remain in the mind and are worth offering to the public as examples of the varied walks of France.

The result is this book, which describes in some (though not exhaustive) detail, twenty of the finest walks in France, a small selection from the great mass of walks available. France has well over twenty-five thousand miles of long-distance footpaths, linked into the network of the *Grande Randonnée*. It might take a lifetime to walk them all, for the GR network is constantly expanding, altering and improving, so some choice, some selection, has to be made.

The selection here is almost entirely arbitrary and personal, but not completely so. Wise writers will remember the advice, 'Do not do unto others as you would have them do unto you; your tastes may not be the same'. What we have here is a selection of walks which should appeal to all kinds of walker.

It might be as well to explain exactly what is intended by a 'Classic Walk'. Walkers' tastes, in terrain, length of journey, and style of walk, will vary immensely, and not every walker is, or would wish to be, a hill-walker or a backpacker. What appeals to one might discourage or bore another. That's the way walkers are, and so be it.

For the purposes of this book, the title must be taken as the definition, and accepted in full. This is a book of Classic Walks in France. Some of the walks are classic by nature of the terrain. The Tour of Mont Blanc, and the GR10

walk across the Pyrénées are examples of this; they would be Classic Walks in any country. Some are classic by historical association, like the Robert Louis Stevenson Trail in the Cévennes, which I had the pleasure of inaugurating in 1978, and which traces the path followed by the Scots writer and his donkey a hundred years before. Some are classic by virtue of the glories they present to the walker, like the GR3 section through the châteaux country of the Loire. All are interesting, none are dull. It is also worth pointing out that French footpaths are designed to display the glories of the countryside, man-made as well as natural. If there is a famous castle or a pretty village on the way, a French footpath will lead you to it. Walking in France is more than an end in itself.

It was a famous Frenchman, the Emperor Napoleon no less, who coined the expression, 'Ask of me anything but time'. It's a heartfelt request for writers as well as soldiers, and to accomplish in time the task of describing twenty footpaths, some assistance was required. I have been joined on this occasion by my good friend and fellow travel writer, David Wickers. David, an experienced walker, sailor, and cross-country skier, has already co-authored a walking book, *Britain at Your Feet,* and is a fair hand with a camera. This book is our first joint project and I look forward to others.

The third member of the triumvirate must be you, the reader. If we have accomplished our task successfully, this book will urge and inspire you to get up from that chair and set out on one of these journeys across the fair face of France. No country in the world has so much to offer the walker — varied terrain, good weather, splendid sights and vast vistas. Even the most committed walker is rarely indifferent to good wine and fine food. It's all there if you are prepared to go out and find it. There are Classic Walks here for walkers of every persuasion, so select one that suits you and go.

Rob Hunter

Vallon-Pont d'Arc (1985)

WALKING

It is said that a person who puts the mugwort plant in his shoes each morning, can walk forty miles before noon without tiring. Don't you believe it. There is no written law which insists that walking holidays have to involve mammoth mileages, compulsory blisters and all-over aches. In fact, the more sedentary your normal lifestyle the more important it is to learn how to be a pedestrian, easing into distances gradually and not over-estimating your capabilities. Miles, or kilometres, are always longer than you think. Besides, there is little point in making 'distance covered' your main criterion because every other single form of transport will put you to shame.

Begin by studying the maps and *Topo-Guides* to build up a picture of the land and a feeling for the terrain, visualising the contours as hills, and allowing for the time that uphill walking and rough going will add to your overall schedule. Robert Louis Stevenson wrote: 'Once you have fallen into an equable stride, it requires no conscious thought from you to keep it up, and yet it prevents you from thinking earnestly of anything else.' The pace to walk at is one that you can keep up for miles and hours at a stretch. Let your rate of breathing determine your walking speed, not the other way round.

As a rough and ready guide, you can reckon on walking about 3mph (5kph) on fairly even ground, if you aren't carrying a pack, and slightly slower if you are. Uphill walking is a slower business, for every 2500ft (800m) of altitude you have to climb, you'll need to add an extra hour to your journey time. Other influences affecting journey time are the weather, the degree of bogginess underfoot, the time taken on rest stops, on photographing the scenery and other such pleasures, unplanned delays such as losing your way and, of course, your own degree of fitness.

On trips lasting more than a few days, it is important to build up distances slowly, taking care not to overdo things on the first day. Everyone's pace must be determined by the slowest member of the group; there is nothing worse than being made to seem a straggler. Pity W.H. Hudson's wife, his frequent walking companion, whom he described as 'the snail in woman's shape'.

If you walk steadily you'll find that a five-minute break every hour should be sufficient for rest and relaxation. Look for shade if it's hot, shelter if it's cold, and enjoy a snack and a drink to keep up your energy level and prevent your body from becoming dehydrated. Big mid-day meals, despite the abundant temptations to be found in rural France, are not conducive to either walking or backpacking; they leave you feeling lethargic and unwilling to press on with the same degree of enthusiasm as in the morning.

Clothing

France, as the largest country in Western Europe, bounded by four seas and a large land mass to the East, is subjected to a far greater variety of climatic influences than Britain, so the variations in weather from one area to another can be enormous. When you are planning a walking trip, it is important to take these regional quirks into account before deciding on your trail clothing.

Climatic records for the French regions taken during the past 60 years show the following periods to be the best for warm, sunny and driest weather (average daytime temperatures)

COAST	WARMEST °C	DRIEST mm
Aquitaine (Biarritz)	June–Sept (17–20)	Mar–July (85–100)
Aquitaine (Bordeaux)	June–Sept (17–20)	Mar–Sept (52–72)
S. Brittany	June–Sept (17–19)	Feb–Oct (45–65)
N. Brittany	June–Sept (14–18)	Mar–Sept (50–80)
Normandy	June–Sept (15–17.5)	Mar–Oct (40–72)
Côte d'Azur/Riviera	May–Oct (16.5–22.5)	Feb–Sept (20–70)
Languedoc-Roussillon	May–Sept (16–22.5)	Jan–Sept (20–70)
North-West France	June–Sept (15.–18.5)	Year round (33–75)
North-East France	June–Sept (15.5–19)	Year round (40–80)
INLAND	WARMEST °C	DRIEST mm
Provence	May–Oct (16.5–22.5)	Mar–Oct (20–75)
Languedoc-Roussillon	May–Oct (16–22.5)	Mar–Oct (20–70)
Midi-Pyrénées	June–Sept (18.5–21.5)	Year round (45–80)
Pyrénées-Atlantique	June–Sept (17.5–20)	June–Sept (56–83)
Dordogne	June–Sept (17–21)	Mar–Sept (45–70)
Auvergne	June–Sept (16.5–19.5)	Year round (20–70)
Rhône Valley	June–Sept (17–21)	Year round (45–88)
Loire Valley	June–Sept (16–19.5)	Year round (45–65)
Burgundy	June–Sept (16–19.5)	Year round (40–80)
Paris	June–Sept (16.5–20)	Year round (45–62)

Clothes are the body's first line of defence against the elements. Pessimistic though this may sound, always prepare for the worst so that you can be sure of staying both warm and dry no matter what the weather decides to hurl your way. Once in France you can hardly pop home for that windproof you left in the wardrobe.

Keeping Warm

Cold is a walker's worst enemy. Humans cannot function properly if their body temperature falls significantly below that magic 98.4°F, so clothing must insulate the body to retain its inner coil warmth even when the outside air temperature falls to freezing or below.

Since the air is a poor conductor of heat, by creating air spaces around the body with layers of clothing, you effectively provide a barrier of still air through which body heat cannot easily escape. Layers of clothing also provide en-route flexibility, enabling you to shed layers as you warm up, replacing them when you stop, *before* you begin to chill.

Don't forget your head, hands and feet. In an attempt to preserve heat the body operates like a thermostat, automatically reducing the flow of blood to the extremities of feet and hands, which are therefore often the first to feel the cold, so that what heat there is gets reserved for the vital organs. The body never starves the brain of blood, and consequently the head loses more than any other part of the body, as much as one third of the body's total heat loss. So, when hands and feet feel cold, be sure to put your hat on, preferably a woollen one.

Wind is a major cause of heat loss, so you must carry a windproof 'shell' garment, either a lightweight poly-cotton/nylon jacket or anorak, to cut the effect of wind chill. (See the chart below to understand the chilling effects of even the mildest breeze.) In the high Alps and Pyrénées the wind chill factor is always relevant.

unless you keep moving. Moisture, a good conductor of heat, takes the place of air in the clothing and body heat can vanish into the surrounding air at an alarming rate.

You need to carry a good quality cagoule or rain parka, plus leggings. The best ones are made from plastic coated with polyurethane or neoprene, and are highly effective, but they do have one adverse side effect. Although they prevent rain reaching you they don't allow body vapour to escape; instead it condenses on the inside surface like steam on a cold bathroom window. On balance though, it is far better to be warm and slightly wet on the inside than wet and very cold all over. The only way to succeed in staying completely dry is to invest in Gore-Tex products which are made from a microporous material able to discriminate between water vapour and rain water, letting the former out but preventing the latter from getting in. Needless to say though, you have to pay considerably more for such miracle materials.

Keeping Cool

In Central and Southern France the summers can be extremely hot. As far as clothing is concerned you will need to wear as little as modesty will permit, although pale skins which burn easily will obviously have to cover up to prevent sunburn, and most people will find a broad-brimmed hat a sensible addition. Cotton tops and baggy shorts will prove the best compromise for the rest of the body.

Wind Chill Chart

WIND SPEED mph	LOCAL TEMPERATURE (C)			
	32	23	14	5
5 (3kph)	29	20	10	1
10 (6kph)	18	7	-4	-15
15 (10kph)	13	-1	-13	-25
20 (12kph)	7	-6	-19	-32
32 (20kph)	1	-13	-27	-41

Remember also the 'lapse rate', by which air temperatures fall as you climb higher, around five Fahrenheit degrees (three Centigrade degrees) for every 1000ft (300m) you ascend. This, too, can be relevant in the high hills of France.

Keeping Dry

The only really disastrous, and potentially dangerous aspect of getting wet is that it invariably involves becoming cold as well,

Boots

When you go walking in France, you and your boots will form the most important relationship in your life, no matter who your travelling companion might be! If you get on badly with your boots, the trip will be ruined.

The type of footwear you need will depend on when and where you are walking. Early spring on the footpaths of Normandy and Brittany, may well mean a series of soggy encounters, so

boots and gaiters are imperative. Similarly, even though the temperature will soar in the summer down south, you will still appreciate the cushioning effect that only a pair of thick boot soles can provide against the stony, rough-and-ready terrain. Thick soles also insulate the feet from the cold ground in winter and take some of the punishment that the weight of a heavy backpack will inflict on tender feet. Don't go to the other extreme and buy heavy-duty mountain clompers. Bear in mind that the 1953 Mount Everest Expedition came to the conclusion that the physical effort of carrying one pound on your feet is the equivalent to an extra five on your back. Don't neglect to consider a good pair of 'trainers' or running shoes either, especially if you can be sure of dry weather conditions. Their thick insoles are likely to give you a comfortable ride over even the roughest terrain, and although boots afford a measure of extra protection for the ankles, both boots and trainers will give you a fair amount of grip on most surfaces. Over most types of terrain, light boots or trainers are sufficient.

You will need advice when buying walking boots for the first time. Go to a specialist outdoor equipment shop. Talk to someone there who knows the business and be prepared to spend a good hour or so trying on different types of footwear and walk around the shop a few times to see what they feel like. Remember to take a pair of suitable socks with you when trying on boots — or borrow a pair from the shop (most outdoor equipment shops keep a thick pair for such purposes), and don't make up your mind until you are confident that your choice of footwear fits like a glove (so to speak). Before you leave the shop ask if they will be prepared to change them after a few days 'test-driving' in the comfort of your own *home*. Don't expect to renegotiate the sale once you have put them to *outdoor* use. That's just *too* much to expect.

No matter how perfect a fit, don't attempt a classic French route in a brand new pair of boots or you will end up with nothing less than a set of classic French blisters. Boots need to be broken-in over a period of time — some say even as much as 500 miles (800km) for a pair of stiff-soled winter-weight boots — before they will stand you in truly comfortable stead.

Backpacking

The classic routes described in this book can be tackled in their entirety in one of two ways. You can either stay in permanent accommodation at hotels, pensions, farmhouses and with favourite aunties, as you travel along the way, or you can camp out, sleeping in either a tent or in one of the many *refuges (gîtes d'étape* or *abris)*, which you will find dotted along the walking trails, especially in the more remote parts of France. Both methods have their advantages. Hotels or *gîtes* mean less weight need be carried, but you will have less freedom; backpacking offers greater flexibility but a heavier load on your back.

The development of such products as polyurethane-coated nylon, lightweight aluminium equipment, mini cooking stoves, synthetic or fibre-pile materials, magnesium alloys, and other high-tech advances in outdoor gear, has made 'getting away from it all' a possibility for people with less-than-bionic bodies. Although such miracles don't come cheaply, they have at least granted people with less than superincomes access to outdoor adventures without the necessity of hiring teams of mules, yaks or Sherpas to transport their daily needs from one overnight location to the next.

The House on Your Back

First things first; before you start gathering all the ingredients needed for a self-sufficient stay in France, buy a backpack to carry them in. The human frame, however slight, is capable of carrying a relatively heavy load with remarkable ease, as long as it is done properly. The principle behind carrying any weight is to keep the load high so that you don't waste any energy in trying to stay and walk upright. Both the modern 'H' frame packs and the contoured 'anatomic' frames allow the weight to be supported both by the shoulders and — with the help of a broad, padded hip-harness — the hips.

When confronted by a vast number of packs on display in the outdoor equipment shops, don't feel that you have to opt for the largest. The size of the pack depends on what you need it for, and if you do go in for excess capacity 'just in case', you will find that it has a nasty habit of absorbing unnecessary items simply because they will fit in the space available, not because you will need them; a variation of Parkinson's Law as applied to the Great Outdoors. Do buy the best quality that you can afford, choosing a well-known brand that has been well tried and tested in rough and remote conditions. A 55-litre sac is about the right size.

Sleeping Bags

When the interior-sprung, duvet-wrapped, king-sized bed lover goes nomadic in France, he or she can still expect to enjoy far more nocturnal comfort than the idea of a mere bag on a thin strip of foam might promise.

Alternatives to the traditional walking boot: The Bionic S walking shoe from Berghaus/Scarpa and the sports boot by Asolo Sports from Karrimor.

The first step towards a good night's sleep is a quality sleeping bag made from a sufficient thickness or 'loft' of down, or the best synthetic filling, to insulate your body from the coldest of nights you are likely to experience. This must also be lightweight and sufficiently compressible so that it does not constitute a ridiculous burden on your back. Good sleeping bags don't come cheaply. Before choosing one, decide on the typical conditions under which it is to be used. You don't need to invest in an expensive, bulky, pure goose-down-filled cocoon, suitable for the Arctic, if you are spending two weeks in summer, ambling through Provence. Talk to the shop assistants and listen to their advice, but decide what you need for yourself.

No matter how luxurious your sleeping bag is, it will still compress under the weight of your body, creating a cold spot with very little insulation between you and the cold ground below. The best remedy for this miserable state is to carry a length of closed-cell mattress, which will neither absorb water like ordinary foam mattress, nor be too heavy to carry like an inflatable air mattress. The *Therm-a-rest* air mattress is a good compromise.

Tents

If you can be *really sure* it isn't going to rain, or become excessively cold and windy, you can sleep *sous les belles étoiles,* in your sleeping bag, on top of your mat, staring up at the heavens. You may well learn, by studying the relevant *Topo-Guide* to your planned walk, that there are sufficient shelters *(abris)* placed at strategic intervals along the route. In all other circumstances you will need a tent.

Despite the phrase 'under canvas', most modern backpacking nights are spent beneath lighter, more durable, less bulky, quicker drying and rot-proof nylon. Such tents come in all shapes and sizes, and prices, but apart from making sure that the one you decide to buy will be large enough to accommodate you, or you and your companion, the choice is very subjective. Don't compromise on quality, or buy one without a fly sheet (since the principle of a 'double roof' is vital in preventing the build-up of condensation) or without a sewn-in ground sheet. Get a good, roomy, lightweight tent, from such proven manufacturers as Ultimate, Vango or Robert Saunders.

An early model of the now popular hoop tent. Current models are spacious and have good wind and rain-shedding capabilities.

Tent Living

Stephen Graham, in *The Gentle Art of Tramping,* recommends that you '... stop where you like, you go on when you like. You surely come to places in which you are tempted to remain ... you linger. And then, when the spirit moves, you move with it, move on, enriched by your delay, by your idleness ...' In order to get the most enrichment from your own idleness, don't leave it too late in the day before stopping for the night. You need plenty of daylight to find somewhere suitable to pitch your tent, if you are not staying on an official site, and to perform all the associated tasks of putting it up, cooking a meal, enjoying the feast, and so on, all of which can turn into a long drawn out farce if you are forced to grope around in pitch dark.

In order to get a good night's sleep you need to be warm, dry and horizontal. If your muscles continually have to compensate for a tendency to slide downhill, however gentle the slope may appear on first inspection, your body will not get the rest it deserves and needs after a full day's tramping. To protect both the groundsheet and your nocturnal well-being, make sure you don't pitch your tent on sharp rocks or knobbly humps. Avoid obvious boggy hollows or water-courses that can flood if there is a heavy downpour during the night.

It is also very convenient to have a nearby source of water, which should be pure or at least able to be purified. The best single clue to such supplies is marked on your map or *Topo Guide.* The chosen tent site should also offer some measure of protection from the wind, such as a hedgerow, wall or contour of land. Finally, take a good look around to make sure that you aren't sharing the site with a handsome, multi-ton Charolais bull, or any other beast; even if normally unaggressive, its inquisitive disposition could lead to a painfully misplaced hoof.

Having found the perfect spot in which to linger, the next priority is to erect the tent. If it happens to be raining, or threatens to do so, the more quickly you can do this the better. This is not the time and place to be erecting your tent for the very first time — your garden at home or the nearby park is the place to practise, following the manufacturer's instructions. Although each tent will differ in the exact procedure to be adopted, most begin by having their floor section pegged down as squarely as you can get it, with no diagonal wrinkles. This will hold the tent in place even if the wind is howling. If the ground is hard, drive the tent pegs home with a rock or the heel of your boot. If that doesn't work, hold down the floor of the

Left: **Lightweight tents** *camping à la ferme* **at the Vallée des Merveilles, in the Alpes-Maritimes.**

Right: **An 'A' Frame Ultimate Tramp tent. Also seen is the Trangier cook set.**

tent with rocks placed along the inside wall and tie the guy lines to convenient trees or walls (which, of course are never to hand in such circumstances).

Point the back of the tent into the prevailing wind. If you pitch broadside the tent will be unstable, with one side continually billowing out and the other in, and if you aim the door towards the wind you will inflate like a balloon and any rain will quickly reach you on the inside. Take the trouble to pitch the tent right first time, as any midnight realignments are a nightmare.

If it is raining, don't clamber into the tent wearing a wet cagoule. Remove outer garments and either leave them in between the fly sheet and the inner wall of the tent or put them into a large plastic bag so that they can't contaminate anything dry. If you are wet beneath your outer layers, get into some dry clothing and, if cold, climb into your sleeping bag. Even if the prospect of putting wet clothes on again the next morning sends shivers down your spine, this is the way it must be. You should always have at least one set of absolutely dry clothing, carried in waterproof plastic bags, ready to wear at night. The rest, if only barely moistened by your body vapours, can be put into a stuff-sac and used as a pillow.

If the late afternoon is still sunny though, the entire experience of camping is vastly improved. You can amble around, take your boots off and slip your feet into something more comfortable, unpack and fluff up your sleeping bag, leaving it to air and 'loft' on the spine of the tent after its day-long confinement, make a mug of tea and start to feel hungry.

Be careful when using your stove. Cooking on a naked flame is the single most dangerous activity when you are camping, so always follow the manufacturer's step-by-step instructions to the letter. Be especially careful if the terrain is tinder dry, as in Corsica, or the *garrigue,* (where, in fact, fires of all kinds, including cigarettes, are frequently outlawed). In particular, position the stove on even ground, well away from anything ignitable, protected from the wind, and *never* use the stove in an unventilated tent. That done, get a brew on and relax.

Moveable Feasts

If this section turns into something disproportionately longer than the rest, we apologise in advance. When walking we both like to eat. We could not, in fact, agree more with William Hazlitt when he wrote in his *On Going On A Journey:* 'Give me the clear blue sky over my

One of the joys of walking in France is the food. *Des huîtres* are a classic dish of Normandy and Brittany.

head and the green turf beneath my feet, a winding road before me and three hours march to dinner ... I laugh, I run, I leap, I sing for joy'. Well, so do we ... almost.

One of the undeniably overwhelming advantages of doing anything in France is the food, and one of the undeniably overwhelming advantages to walking there, on these classic routes, is the justification for such indulgences. A full day's hiking along even a level footpath will burn around 1500 calories or more on top of your basic metabolic rate. Carry a 25-lb (11-kg) to 30-lb (14-kg) pack on your back and the richest of culinary sauces will not be translated into circumference around your waistline. If, on the other hand, you intend carrying a backpack in order to remain relatively self-sufficient, either to keep the holiday budget within acceptable bounds or to walk in areas of the country where there are few shops and restaurants are as real as the mirage of *cassoulet* to a ravenous hiker, then you will need to carry your own DIY gastronomy kit.

When deciding on the food to take on a backpacking trip, there are three things to consider: quantity, nutritive value, and taste. Walking, as we have already stressed, increases your body's demand for food above the usual intake, especially if your normal daily existence tends to be highly sedentary. It is impossible to provide hard and fast rules about specific quantities, since this depends on a score of variables, including body weight and metabolism, the weight you are carrying, the number of uphill gradients, distance travelled, air temperature, and so on. However, an *average* walker will need somewhere in the region of 3,500 to 4,000 calories a day, the equivalent, approximately, of $1\frac{1}{2}$lb to 2lb (1kg) of food. If you don't consume sufficient for your needs you won't have enough energy which means, at best, that you will soon become tired, and at worst, it could result in total exhaustion, a potentially dangerous state to find yourself in on a wild winter's day, a long way from shelter.

John Muir, the great American conservationist and founder of the Sierra Club, was a fierce advocate of travelling light, and would spend days on end in the wilderness, sustained merely by a few pocketfuls of rice. The longer you have to be dependent upon the food you carry, the greater the importance of a well balanced diet. This must include a proper intake of vitamins, proteins, minerals and fats as well as carbohydrates. There is no need to become obsessed by diet, but do use common sense and include plenty of nuts, grains, dried fruits, seeds, cheese, dried milk, pulses and dehydrated vegetables in your pack, all of which are low in cost, weight and bulk but high in calorific energy.

The nearest you are likely to come to the kind of food normally enjoyed while at home, is the pre-packed, fully pre-prepared meal made by a number of specialist firms. The 'menus' can sound like a cosmopolitan restuarant, although the actual taste of your average *boeuf stroganoff* or *chili con carne* may be a lot more disappointing than the promise on the packet. The great advantage of the pre-packaged meal is that it is extremely light to carry, will keep for ages without deterioration, and is easily prepared by the one-pot, boiling water method.

When choosing your outdoor menu, do read the labels carefully, avoiding dishes that demand a lot of simmering time (thereby draining your fuel and water supplies) and compare the weights and prices of the various makes. An alternative to the convenient but relatively expensive pre-packed meal is to simply buy and carry all the ingredients. Stock cubes or packet soups can form the liquid base, pasta, rice, dried potato or lentils the bulk, and dehydrated vegetables the essential taste, boosted by vital herbs, spices (especially curry), seasoning and other gourmet touches. Contrary to what the 'broken egg, burnt sausages and beans in a billy' brigade would have you believe, camp site meals can be highly creative and satisfying experiences.

Cooking Stoves

An enormous range of cooking stoves are now available to the outdoor enthusiast, each with its particular set of pros and cons and stalwart aficionados. Butane gas is one of the most popular fuels since the stove is so light to carry, easy to light, control and re-fuel, clean to use, and the cartridges are widely available both in the U.K. and in France for example, *Camping Gaz*. The main disadvantage is the need to carry the empty cartridges around until they can be properly disposed of. Butane gas also tends to behave in a fickle manner when the temperature falls, and not at all when it drops below freezing.

Petrol stoves are an old favourite, notably the *Optimus* or *SVEA 123*. They are expensive to buy but relatively cheap to run; they are also less convenient to use than gas since they need to be primed by pre-heating the vapourising tube so creating the needed pressure. Since petrol is both highly volatile and its fumes toxic, such stoves must be treated with a great deal of respect, as outlined in all manufacturers' instructions.

Paraffin stoves operate along similar lines to petrol and share the advantage of burning very hot, but they often need to be primed or pumped while cooking in order to maintain pressure. Methylated spirit stoves burn silently and without the need to build up any pressure, although the fuel is both costly and may be difficult to come by in parts of France. The real choice, therefore, lies between gas and petrol stoves.

Stoves and fuel supplies apart, the rest of the *batterie de cuisine* should be kept to a bare minimum. One lidded pot will generally be sufficient. You will also need a pot grip (an advisable extra even if the pot is fitted with a handle), a pint mug which can double both for eating and drinking, a spoon, a large plastic water bottle, a can opener, a small knife (ideally a single, self-locking blade or a Swiss army officer's knife with a minimum range of gadgets) and, ready for the celebratory *Château Lafite,* a corkscrew.

Packing a Backpack

Robert Louis Stevenson, one of history's more ardent walkers, once wrote that: 'During the first day or so of any tour there are moments of bitterness when the traveller feels more coldly towards his knapsack, when he is half a mind to throw it bodily over the hedge ... and yet it soon acquires a property of easiness. It becomes magnetic; the spirit of the journey enters into it.' Carry too much weight and you will find that any rapport you share will lie only with

Brewing up on a Camping Gaz stove using the pack as a windbreak.

French students rest their H-frame packs while discussing their route through the wine country.

Even in summer, high altitude weather can be unpredictable. Always set out prepared for the worst.

Stevenson's early thoughts.

What you must take must be determined by what you *need* and not by what your pack will hold. Paul Petzoldt, the American wilderness expert, cleverly suggests that just before you pack, you make two piles, one containing things classed as 'absolutely necessary', and the other 'things that might be needed.' You then totally reject the latter pile and turn your energies towards whittling down the first.

Unless you are built like an ox and are in top physical condition, don't exceed 30-35lb (14-16kg), and far less if you are starting out for the first time. Pack the heaviest objects on top and towards the back of the pack so that the weight is carried towards the top of the spine, as near to the centre of gravity as possible. However waterproof your backpack is supposed to be, all items of equipment which need to be kept dry, especially spare clothing, sleeping bag, food (with each meal packed into individual bags) and of course toilet paper, must be packed into plastic bags.

Pack systematically. If you know, more or less, where everything is, you won't need to turn the entire pack load upside down every time you want something. Things you need to get at quickly should be packed in the top or side pockets, including cagoules, maps and guides, spare sweater, hat, gloves, jacket, camera, trail nibbles, and so on.

Maps

French topographic maps are produced to various scales by the Institut Géographique National, the French equivalent of the Ordnance Survey. Their 1:50,000 (1¼ins = 1 mile) scale is used to illustrate the walks in the FFRP *Topo guides,* but walkers may also wish to use the IGN 1:100,000 scale 'Green' *Carte Verte* or the 1:50,000 (1¼ins = mile) or 1:25,000 (2.5ins = 1 mile). These can be obtained from various shops in France, or from the IGN shop in Paris, just off the Champs-Elysées, or in the U.K. from Stanfords Ltd., or MacCarta Ltd., the IGN agent in Britain (who operate a mail order service), both of whom are in London. (See appendices for addresses.)

Map and Compass

Once you know how to use it, a compass can keep you on the right trail wherever there is a point of confusion, and help you find your way across-country, away from the defined routes. Since one end of the needle on the compass always points to the north, you can transfer this information to your map and 'set' it so that it is aligned in the proper direction, corresponding to the lie of the land. Such a tool is infinitely more reliable than any human 'sense' of direction and should always be trusted. Walking in wild country, trusting to your 'sense of direction' is a sure way to get lost. Trust your compass.

The compass you need for walking is a protractor type, such as those produced by Silva. Each one comes with a set of comprehensive, well-written instructions, so there is no need to waste words here, describing how to use it — but if you cannot read a map and use a compass, learn before you set out on the wilder classic walks.

Weather Wisdom

John Ruskin maintained that: 'There is really no such thing as bad weather, only different kinds of good weather'. To sustain such optimism you must always travel prepared for the worst, so that you can stay warm and dry no matter how severe the elements may be.

We have already dealt with the importance of carrying good quality, weatherproof clothing. When the trip involves overnight camping it is not only important that your sleeping bag is adequate for the likely conditions you will encounter, but also that it is kept dry enough to serve its purpose. If the worst should happen and you and everything in your pack is transformed into a single, soggy mess, a dry sleeping bag will at least guarantee a warm and comfortable night. Synthetic-filled bags offer some measure of protection when wet, but down is absolutely useless when wet as the feathers matt together and lose their insulating properties. So always double-wrap bags in sealed plastic bags. Don't just rely on the nylon stuff-sac that comes with the sleeping bag.

If keeping dry is the first rule of wet weather walking, drying out whatever gets wet is the second. Grab whatever opportunity you can during the day to dry off your clothing and equipment. If the sun appears try to find time to stop, air your sleeping bag, spread out all other wet items on branches, fences and walls, (and generally transform the delightful French *campagne* into a *temporary* garbage tip). Another more unsightly, though immensely practical tip, is to dry out smaller items, like socks, while you are on the move by tying them to the back of your pack.

Winter Wonderlanding

Not all walks have to be made in the summer. We both like rambling on cross-country skis, and Rob is always raving about his travels in the Aubrac. Walking trips during the winter months have their own very special rewards. Apart from the stark, depopulated and often snow-white beauty of the scenery, the expected discomforts can easily be offset by having the right equipment and any potential hazards averted by knowing just what you are doing. Winter can, by the same token, be a highly

Above: **White-out conditions, since they obliterate all recognisable land forms, make a compass indispensable.**

Below: **Travelling by skis or snow shoes may be the only way to travel across a winter landscape.**

demanding experience, especially on the country's higher ground, so if you have any doubts as to your degree of fitness or lack of experience, think twice before making such off-season commitments. Stick to three-season walks until you have plenty of experience.

In order to be able to stay warm and dry when the winter weather is at its worst, you obviously will need to carry plenty of extra clothing, double-wrapped in plastic bags to keep dry (tedious though this repetitive advice will sound) plus plenty of food and warm overnight gear, including a thicker sleeping bag if you are sleeping out. Other items likely to come into their own during a winter walk are gaiters (when travelling through areas which receive heavy rainfalls or snow), heavier, more insulating footwear, and high-energy food snacks.

Deep-lying snow rules out walking, except for those who wear snow-shoes, but if the coating is fairly thin (up to two or three inches) it will only become a problem where you encounter steep gradients. Resist the natural tendency to lean towards a slope, as this makes an unwelcome slip more likely. You will generally find it easier to zig-zag up the side of a hill using the edge of your boot to avoid sliding, keeping your legs straight when descending, plunging your heels into the snow.

The more hilly the countryside the more caution you need to exercise and the more necessary it becomes to carry, *and know how to use,* an ice-axe, both as a 'third leg' and as a self-arrest device in a slide. You must learn to master this technique *before* you need to use it, preferably coached first-hand by an expert in a place where failure to do it properly will not send you hurtling down onto a host of exposed rocks.

Finally, one of the other 'adverse' side effects of fallen snow is that the well-posted, well-trodden *Grande Randonnée* waymarks may become obliterated. Your skills with both map and compass therefore become all the more important since a navigational error could so easily lead to problems.

Trouble-Shooting

Your feet are more likely to let you down than any other part of your body. More trips are ruined on account of blisters than any other single cause, but they can be easily prevented. Blisters have a considerate habit of letting you know they are on their way long before they get an inflated sense of self-importance. If you feel a hint of soreness, aptly described as a 'hot spot', deal with it *immediately*. It won't go away of its own accord. Stop, remove your boot and

sock, and apply a patch of 'Moleskin' on the reddened area. 'Moleskin' is available from most large chemist shops.

The second most frequent hazard is sunburn and lip-burn. The French summer can be very hot and the sun can burn with the intensity of a furnace. At the best of times, sunburn can be agonising, but it is doubly debilitating if you try to carry on with your walking plans as if nothing has happened. Fair-skinned walkers should be particularly wary and wear a brimmed cotton hat, cover any exposed neck area with a bandana or neckerchief, and generously smear exposed parts of the body, neck, wrists, backs of hands, with a high factor sunscreen, certainly in the early days of the walk. Use a lip-salve to stop blistering and apply more of it at regular intervals when needed. It is also vital that you don't allow your body to dehydrate, a state which can readily occur in hot weather. Drink frequently and take advantage of any streams or fountains to give your body a cool bathe.

Surviving

Once you have begun a trip, no matter how committed you are to a schedule, always be prepared to modify your plans if the weather deteriorates or you begin to feel exhausted. Walking is supposed to be fun, not a survival course. Remember that wet-cold is the Number One enemy, so the basic necessities of survival centre around being able to stay warm and dry.

Get into the habit of carrying some emergency gear, even on a day outing in the high hills. If you do get lost, exhausted, ravaged by bad weather, or injured, you may have to spend an unplanned night in the open. That doesn't mean carrying a full camper's kit all the time 'just in case', but you should always have some spare clothing and some high energy emergency rations (chocolate, cheese, nuts or special outdoor survival food items) which you must swear never to dip into except in times of need. An indispensable item of equipment, and one that takes up little room or weight in a pack, is a 'bivvy' (short for bivouac) survival bag. It is simply a large, body-size, sack made of thick polythene, but it will protect you from the worst of the elements.

It is beyond the scope of this book to detail all the nasty things that *could* conceivably happen, even on a classic walk in France, as well as lending an unnecessarily gloomy tone to the book. If you do want to walk, confident in your abilities to cope with all emergencies, there is no short cut other than enrolling in a proper Red Cross or St John Ambulance Brigade first-aid course, followed by one in Mountain Leadership skills — but you don't *need* to go as far as that. The basic skills which all walkers should know are covered in a number of books listed in the bibliography. If you don't want to expose yourself to any risks whatsoever, then stay at home and walk through the pages of this book from the comfort and security of your favourite armchair; but you will miss more than a lot, and most of what you will miss will be the fun.

This chapter is mainly a basic *aide-mémoire* to walking on long-distance footpaths — so if you know about the basics, let us now look at the footpaths of France.

Rob Hunter well-equipped for the severe conditions that surround him. A hat and gloves would also be carried.

WALKING IN FRANCE

The valley of the Tarn offers spectacular scenery and excellent walking.

Any wise walker will have gained at least a little experience walking at home, before crossing the Channel and tackling one of those longer, higher and very often warmer footpaths that criss-cross the fair land of France. The fact that France is overseas, and not the place one would pop to for a quick stroll on a Sunday afternoon, should also concentrate the mind. Any walk in France inevitably becomes a kind of expedition, demanding a certain tenacity and at least a week of your time if anything worthwhile is to be attempted or accomplished. It follows therefore, that a walking trip to France has to be *planned* and the purpose of this chapter is firstly to explain the nature of those facilities and or-ganisations open to the walker in France or the U.K., and secondly, to indicate reliable sources of sound information, for good information is

the basis of all successful plans. Last, but by no means least, to point out the areas in which walking in France differs from walking in the U.K. — or indeed anywhere else. In practice, the differences are very few but the fact that they exist needs to be considered. France is not Britain, or the U.S.A. It is a country apart, marching to a different, Gallic, drummer, and the walker in France, unshielded by train, or car, or package tour, may experience this dif-ference more closely than other kinds of travel-ler; but then I would add *Vive la Différence* at any time. It is also only proper to point out that anyone setting out to walk in France must be prepared for a little give and take with the local population.

Even on the best organised expeditions, things can still go wrong, and if they did not, life would be much duller than it is. However, it is still vital to have a good plan, and the effort which goes into making the plan not only contributes to the success of the walk, but can also be great fun in itself. The basis of any sensible plan is accurate, reliable and up-to-date information. Do not neglect to acquire it, check it and, in the end, use it.

Why France?

Before setting out to unravel the intricacies of walking in France, it might be reasonable to enquire why anyone should go walking in France at all. It is, let's face it, full of Frenchmen, and they are not usually counted among the most agreeable people on earth. Ducking that point for the moment, the simplest answer to the direct question, 'Why walk in France?' is to reply that France contains more of what walkers want, and of a higher quality, than almost anywhere else on earth, with the added bonus of being not too far away from Britain. To get from anywhere in Britain to the furthest-flung footpath of France, the Trans-Corsica GR20, need take no more than a day.

Then consider a country which has thousands of miles of footpath, in a relatively empty but always glorious countryside: two mountain ranges in the Alps and the Pyrénées, and such lesser but magnificent regions as the Cévennes, the Ardèche and the Massif Central. The climate, certainly south of the Loire, is hot and dry for most of the year, and the countryside is full of good food, awash with good wine, and even today, marvellously inexpensive.

Consider all these, and 'Why France?' becomes easy to answer, but above all, France is different and France is ABROAD. That alone can make the shortest walk an adventure, but France has walks for all kinds of walker, from those interested in history to those unhappy souls who need a 'challenge'. Those who try walking in France once, rapidly become addicted, and have to go there again and again.

Finally, and not to duck the issue in the end, let us consider the French. To those who love France and take the trouble to learn a little French, few people are more pleasant, or if they put their minds to it, more obnoxious, than the French. Walkers, however, will meet the country people of France, a very different kind from those encountered driving Paris taxis, or working in up-market hotels. The country people of France are hospitable, kind, delightful and always helpful to those walkers who make the effort to be friendly in return. If you speak a little French, so much the better. The French are not homogenous, and the walker will encounter French Basques, Bretons, Auvergnats,

Normans, to name but a few, all different, all French, all friendly if *you* make the aforesaid effort and are prepared to meet them halfway; but now let us look at their country in detail.

The Loire valley offers a gentle introduction to walking in France whilst the *châteaux* contribute to the picturesque scenery.

Terrain

Metropolitan France is the largest country in Western Europe. It covers, in all, an area of some 220,000 square miles (550,000 square kilometres), roughly three times the area of Britain. The population of France is largely concentrated in the northern regions around Paris and the industrial parts of Artois and Lorraine and along the Mediterranean coast, with only a few cities, Bordeaux, Lyon, Toulouse or Marseille, having populations in excess of half-a-million. This all adds up to a countryside which is, by British standards, empty of people and largely unspoiled.

The countryside of France is also very varied and can offer, on one extreme, the vast flatlands of the Landes on the Atlantic Coast, or the great plain of the Beauce, south of Paris, and on the other, the snow-clad heights of Mont Blanc, which at 1465ft (4807m) is the highest peak in Europe.

Traditionally, the most popular areas for walking in France are the Alps, the Pyrénées, and the Massif Central. All these are hill walking areas, but as the footpath network of the *Grande Randonnée* continues to expand, more and more areas are coming into use and fashion. The lesser-known Cévennes and Ardèche have attracted large numbers of walkers over the last few years, while the Corbières foothills of the Pyrénées, the high plateau of the Cerdagne, the Morvan forest of Burgundy, the great valley of the Loire, or any of the National Parks are, in their various ways, ideal for walking.

We all have our own particular favourites when we think of suitable walking areas. That's our privilege. However, in writing a book on walking we have to consider other kinds of walking and walkers, and so here, as we move across France by these classic trails, we must encounter a great variety of walking terrain.

To give the broad picture, France becomes hotter, more rugged and mountainous as the traveller moves south and east. The north of France, Brittany, Normandy and the Ile de France, are really no more than rolling, and are made up for the most part of agreeable farming country, a mixture of field and forest, though this broad picture must exempt the vast forests of the Ile de France, the rocky hills of the Suisse Normande and the jagged coast of Finistère. Further east, beyond Champagne, lie the Ardennes, but the land to the south of Paris stays fairly placid into Burgundy, after which it soars into glory in the Auvergne, where there is good hill walking everywhere, and real mountains too, often snow-tipped in winter. Walkers here will enjoy the Velay, the Aubrac plateau, anywhere around the Puy de Sancy 5750ft (1885m) or the volcano country east of the town of Clermont-Ferrand.

South of the Massif Central lies the Dordogne, the high plateaux of Quercy and a host of lesser hills, the Cévennes, the Espinouse, the Fenouillèdes, the Corbières, each the foothills or outcrops of the real mountain ranges of France, the Alps and the Pyrénées. Those who like flatter country must stay to the west, in the Vendée, Aquitaine or in parts of the Basque country; but wherever you go in France, the scenery is always attractive and usually quite superb.

Climate

Taken as a whole, France enjoys good weather. There is a variety of climate which is influenced by three main weather systems, the Atlantic, the Mediterranean, and the Continental, but it should be accepted by those more used to the temperate or (to put it another way) unreliable British weather, that the weather in France is at once more reliable, and more extreme. Only a fool would become dogmatic about European weather but *as a rule* the weather north of the Loire tends to be similar to that of southern Britain, becoming perceptibly drier east of Paris, at least as far as the Alps.

To find good and *reliable* summer weather it is best to go south of the Loire, but the weather there does tend to extremes and it can get very hot indeed, with temperatures in the 80s°F (upper 20s°C) or even higher for days or weeks at a time during the summer months. Such heat can be very exhausting to those travelling on foot, and especially to those on backpacking trips.

In winter, northern France, Picardy, Artois, the Ardennes, can be dreary, but the greater height of the French hills leads to the precipitation falling as snow anywhere in the east or south, certainly anywhere over, say, 2000ft (600m). This snow can come early and stay late. I have been driven off the Pyrénées by a blizzard in October, seen snow on the Col de Tourmalet in July, and one photographic expedition for this book was hampered by September snowstorms in the Auvergne and in the Alps around Chamonix.

Simply from the point of view of climate the best months for walking in France are April, May, June, September and October. Even then the wise walker will consider the problems created by heat, or late snow on the tops, and be prepared to adjust the travel plans accordingly. Climate and terrain have to be considered *together* and, although both will vary from one region to another, the walker should remember that in France the mountains are higher, the sun hotter, and the snow arrives earlier and stays later than it tends to do in Britain. This fact will also affect the choice of clothing and equipment. Suncream, lipsalve, and shorts, ice-axes and crampons, may be listed as essential items on some walks, and often at those times of the year when they would be quite unnecessary in Britain.

The Footpath Network

France has at least a hundred thousand miles of country footpaths. The glory of this network, and the finest parts of France are all on the route of that marvellous composition, the long-distance footpaths of the *Grande Randonnée*. The *Grande Randonnée* is expanding quickly but it currently includes over 18,000 miles (30,000km) of waymarked long-distance footpath, split into some two hundred separate though often interlinked footpaths, long or short.

This is only an approximate figure because the network is expanding all the time, under the supervision of the *Fédération Française de la Randonnée Pédestre — Comité National des Sentiers de la Grande Randonnée,* which is more usually abbreviated to CNSGR. A *sentier* is a footpath, and so a *Sentier de la Grande Randonnée* is a long-distance footpath. All the walks in this book, with the exception of the Robert Louis Stevenson Trail, are footpaths on the *Grande Randonnée* (GR), a term which is generally used to describe the long-distance footpaths as a whole.

All GR footpaths are named and numbered, so that the long-distance footpath on the Pilgrim Road from Le Puy, for example, is catalogued and waymarked as the GR65, *Chemin de St Jacques de Compostelle* and, since it is a very long path, it takes no less than five *Topo-Guides* or guidebooks, to describe this Way in detail.

Apart from these main GR trails, walkers can also encounter *GR de Pays,* regional paths which are sometimes (but not always) adopted by the CNSGR; *Sentiers de PR (Petite Randonnée),* which are short local footpaths; and in certain remote parts of the South, *drailles,* or drove-roads. It is advisable to point out that these footpaths are established and waymarked by local branches of the FFRP-CNSGR, and since their accuracy and enthusiam varies, and the links between these branches and the central body are not always close, it is sometimes difficult to establish exactly what is happening on any footpath at any particular time, for the network is altering a little all the time as diversions (*variantes*) are incorporated into the main route, or added, or split off to become footpaths in their own right. However, France is like that; anyone expecting common accord and uniformity is doomed to frustration. Remember

Vive la différence, and look to your maps.

Two final points. Firstly, to provide a good walk for the walker with two or three weeks to spare, we have selected either walks which may be comfortably completed in that time, or that section of a long walk which is, in our opinion, the most attractive or most typical of the walk as a whole. Finally, French footpaths always incorporate the best of what lies on the way, and will wind and wander to deliver the walker to the finest viewpoint, or at the gates of a splendid

WAYMARKS			CONVENTIONAL SIGNS	
GRANDE RANDONÉE PATH		**DIVERSION** Indicates a waymarked trail–off the main path– to visit a historic site, viewpoint etc.		Station
STRAIGHT AHEAD		DIVERSION		Bus Stop
				Hostel (no warden)
				Hostel (with warden)
				Campsite
				Food Shop
				Restaurant
				Snack Bar
CHANGE OF DIRECTION		CHANGE OF DIRECTION PLUS DIVERSION		Water Tap
				Beauty Spot

SIGN BOARD INDICATING GR NUMBER

TOURISME PEDESTRE
SENTIER
G.R. 9

WRONG WAY!

No waymarks for 750 m

750 m

DISTANCE SIGNPOSTS

G.R. 1 ORRY LA-VILLE: 5 km

SEUGY: 11 km

The various waymarks that will be found on the *Sentiers de la Grande Randonnée.*

château. It is often possible to cut corners, but to see it all, stay with the path and follow the *Topo-Guide*.

The Law for Walkers

Those British walkers who have clashed with landowners or the farming community at home will find the country folk of France a very different and far more friendly people. There is, of course, far more space and the land is not farmed as intensively, but national attitudes have a lot to do with it. The French see themselves as individuals, and as individualists. The walker, therefore, is another individual and his or her rights must also be respected. Provided the walkers are friendly, the country people will be happy to welcome them and allow them to walk across their land.

As a general rule the walker is free to wander on any footpath and open track. Property is private if clearly surrounded by a ditch, fence or wall and marked *Propriété Privée*. Obviously walkers will avoid trampling on growing crops, picking fruit or scaring livestock. Some tracks are gated or fenced to stop livestock straying, but walkers are still permitted to pass *(toléré)*. Signs such as *Réserve de Chasse* or *Chasse Privée*, simply mean that the shooting is reserved for the owner and his friends.

Different rules apply in the National and Regional Parks, all of which are popular walking areas. The most common is that all camping must be on official sites, especially if within one hour's walk of a road or under 4,500ft (1.500m) in height. In practice, provided the walker leaves no litter and is careful with cigarettes and fires, there will usually be no problem. Because of the fire risk, camping is not permitted in many of the southern woods or forests, and *not at all* in Corsican forests during the summer months.

Finally, walkers should know and comply with the tenets of the French Country Code.

Country Code *(Côde du Randonneur)*

1. Love and respect Nature.
2. Avoid unnecessary noise.
3. Destroy nothing.
4. Do not leave litter.
5. Do not pick flowers or plants.
6. Do not disturb wildlife.
7. Re-close all gates.
8. Protect and preserve the habitat.
9. No smoking or fires in the forests. (This rule is essential and actively enforced).
10. Stay on the footpath.
11. Respect and understand the country way of life and the country people.
12. Think of others as you think of yourself.

National Parks

France has a very large number of National and Regional Parks, and the parks themselves are often extensive, covering many hundreds of square miles of countryside. They are best regarded as similar to our National Parks found in Britain, rather than as places frozen in time, because people live, work and farm in them, very much as they always have. The only real change is that commercial and industrial development is forbidden, or at least severely restricted, while the facilities for certain types of tourism, usually of the kind connected with outdoor activities, are being steadily but discreetly improved, notably with the increasing provision of *gîtes d'étape* and *chambres d'hôte* facilities. Any walker seeking somewhere lovely to explore should consider wandering in a National Park. A list of the National Parks is given in the appendices.

Maps and Guides

One thing which every walker needs is a good map, and fortunately French mapping is excellent. The basic tool for any walker following a route in this book is the relevant CNSGR *Topo-Guide*, mapped to the 1:50,000 scale ($1\frac{1}{4}$in = 1 mile). Those needed for any particular walk are given at the start of each description. In addition, walkers may feel the need to use a map, and here again, a wide variety of scales is available, usually in the maps published by the Institut Géographique National (IGN).

The basic tool for planning a walk in France is the IGN Map No. 903 *Sentiers de la Grande Randonnées*, which gives the current position of the overall footpath network. For use on the ground, the IGN *Carte Verte* 1:100,000 (1cm = 10km) is excellent, and the IGN also produce metric maps of the 1:50,000 ($1\frac{1}{4}$in = 1 mile) and 1:25,000 ($2\frac{1}{2}$ins = 1 mile), which show all the footpaths, contours and so on. For walking most GR trails, the *Topo-Guide* and the *Carte Verte* are quite adequate.

Apart from the IGN maps, others are produced by Michelin, and the Grenoble publishers Didier-et-Richard, who have produced an excellent series of maps for walks in the Alps and Jura, showing the waymarked trails. Care must be exercised in two areas when using French maps. Generally, the contour interval is 20m on the 1:50,000 and 10m on the 1:25,000. However, on some maps, notably the Didier-et-Richard, *both* scales are used, which can be confusing. Most topographic maps will give the local magnetic variation *(déclinaison magnétique)*, which naturally varies across

France. Where it is not given, but we need to use the compass, we usually set 5°W, which is normally right to within one or two degrees. However, and especially in the mountains, it is best to discover the accurate variation wherever possible. With the *Topo-Guide,* a map, a compass, and good waymarking of the path, following the route is usually the least of the problems.

Apart from these three well-established map-makers, IGN, Michelin and Didier-et-Richard, there is a great deal of derivative mapping about, often produced by the walking clubs or by tourist boards, to supplement the wealth of information given in the local guidebooks.

When it comes to guidebooks, the walker is again well blessed. Apart from the basic tools of CNSGR *Topo-Guides* and IGN 1:100,000 maps, guide books in French or English are produced by Fayard, Didier-et-Richard, the Club Alpin Français (CAF), and the Randonnées Pyrénéennes, as well as small U.K. publishers such as the West Col, Cicerone Press and others. These are available direct from the publishers or from such established sources as Stanfords or MacCarta in London.

It is most important to get up-to-date maps and guides. Note the date of publication on whichever map or guide you have obtained, for all information, however definitive, is subject to change.

Fortunately in France the situation is improving all the time, so any dated information is likely to be on the minimum facilities available, while the current situation you will find on the ground is usually even better.

Accommodation

The walker in France will find a wide variety of accommodation available, at a price which always offers good value for money and is often amazingly cheap by British standards. This can range from four- or five-star *Grand Hôtel de Luxe* to a *Logis* or *Auberge* (a family-run hotel) to a *gîte d'étape* (an unmanned hostel), a *routier* (cafe), an *auberge de jeunesse* (Youth Hostel), a *refuge* (a hut), an *abri* (shelter), a *chambre d'hôte* (bed and breakfast), a *camping* (camp site), *camping à la ferme* (a farm camp site), or *camping sauvage* and *à la belle étoile* (wild camping). As you can see, the choice is vast.

Hotels are common, even in country districts. The best ones for walkers are those belonging to the network of *Auberges et Logis de France,* family-run hotels serving local food, and very inexpensive. In any hotel the price is displayed both in the foyer *and* behind the room door, and the price includes the listed facility — shower

(douche), or bath *(bain),* but not breakfast. Always inspect the room before accepting it — and the pillows are in the wardrobe.

Gîtes d'étape will be very useful to the walker, for they are now being opened along all the GR trails. The standards vary but all offer simple but adequate accommodation, with bunks, showers, a stove, and hot water. They are open to all with a limited stay of two or three nights, and are very cheap, about 20 francs (£2) a night currently. Youth Hostels are not common in the French countryside but all the high hills and

Above: **A mountain *refuge* in the Vercors, Dauphiné.**

Below: **A typical *gîte* on the GR9 in the Haut Buguy.**

Examples of the unofficial signposting that occurs all over the French countryside.

mountains are equipped with huts or shelters *(abris)*, often run or provided by the Club Alpin Francais or the local footpath group. Some are lavish, and have a warden *(le gardien)*, some are frankly primitive. Members of the CAF or an affiliate such as the U.K. branch of the Austrian Alpine Club, are allowed to reserve accommodation and will pay a lower fee. Others have to take the chance that space is available, or sleep on the floor. *Routier* cafes are designed to cater for lorry drivers and not all have accommodation, but all offer good, cheap meals and many do, in fact, have rooms. Bed and Breakfast accommodation is increasingly available in the small villages, and walkers should enquire at the local café or post office if no *'chambre d'hôte'* sign is visible.

Camp sites vary from the very lavish down to the cold water tap and earth closet. Even if the site is said to be full *(complet)*, it is worth enquiring about space, for a pitch just large enough to take a small backpacking tent can often be found. *Camping à la ferme* signs abound in the French countryside, but those who wish to camp wild should attempt to find the landowner and ask permission before pitching. The big worry with wild pitching, as far as the local people are concerned, is fire, so wild camping is actually prohibited in Languedoc, Provence and Corsica, or indeed anywhere risky during the tinder-dry months of summer.

Sources of Information

Before proceeding to suggest how any chosen walk might be planned and executed, some mention must be made of sources of information. Any good trip depends on a good plan, and any good plan depends on accurate, up-to-date information. For this reason, and because all books take about two years to research, write and publish, and will then stay in print for some years after that, we have chosen to give general advice and sources rather than present particular facts which are bound to date or change. We have made this point before, but it is worth restating.

Walkers should cast about widely for information, gleaning as many facts as possible from people who live in or near the area they intend to visit, or from those who have been there recently. This information can be gathered from tourist authorities in the U.K. or France, from the various regional offices, from walking organisations of France and England, from magazines, books, even photographs. The best way to collect such information is to draw up an *Outline Plan* for your trip and then contact all those people who need to have that particular piece of information for their own use.

Information can therefore be gathered from such sources as: British Rail Information Offices, Ferry Companies, Airlines, Books, Magazines, Maps, Tourist Offices and Tour Operators, especially those concerned with outdoor travel and walking. To such U.K. sources must be added the even more extensive facilities available in France, both through the regional or provincial Offices of Tourism, the local *Syndicat d'Initiative*, which can be found in all towns and most villages, and those major national and regional organisations concerned with open-air activities *(activités de plein air)*, such as ABRI in Brittany, CHAMINA in the Auvergne, the Club Vosgian in Alsace Lorraine, and the Randonnée Pyrénéenne in the south. If possible, any outward journey should be routed via one of their offices, so that the visitor can get any relevant and up-to-date information and advice. A full list of such sources is given in the appendices, but the starting point for all visits to France, on foot or otherwise, is the French Government Tourist Office (FGTO). Any request for information to the FGTO should be specific, and include at least 50p in stamps on a self-addressed envelope.

Walkers' Organisations

Many ardent Francophiles have travelled in France for years before it occurred to them that they could see more of the country if they abandoned their cars and the package tour, and started to explore France on foot. It is necessary to explain therefore, that rural France is completely covered with a network of organisations all more or less interested in walking, many seeing it as a way to attract useful and much needed life and revenue back into the under-populated rural areas. Some of these organisations have already been mentioned, such as the FFPR-CNSGR, and the provincial clubs like ABRI and CHAMINA, and the Club Vosgian and a full list is given in the appendices. They have a very direct involvement in promoting walking, but the activity does not stop there. Since *gîtes* are necessary, and often found on farms, the local *Chambre d'Agriculture* is often involved. The *Syndicats d'Initiative,* or local tourist offices, are now actively waymarking their local paths, and improving those sections of the longer National GR routes which pass through their areas. At every stage and level these regional and local organisations are producing maps and guide books.

Walkers planning an extended tour therefore has no lack of sources. They can begin with the FGTO and those U.K. organisations associated with travelling to France. Within France the CNSGR-FFRP in Paris offers the national picture. Below this lie the larger clubs and the provincial footpath organisations, and at the end, on the ground, are the *Syndicats,* the *gîtes,* the camp sites, the waymarked trails. The only snag with all this is that the information these people produce is often conflicting. For this book we gathered together all the available documentation, from every source we know, an amount which filled three tea-chests. We then checked it out and where differences existed, attempted to rationalise them down to an accurate and balanced picture. However, any wise walker will always up-date any information whenever possible, and call on every source available to do so. Do not be too surprised to find the situation you encounter is just a little different. *Vive la ...* etc.

The Administrative Structure of France

Readers must appreciate that France is not Britain. This may seem a blinding glimpse of the obvious, but we have learned from bitter experience that many people expect France to be just like England with a foreign accent and are mightily surprised to discover that it is not like that at all. Their next assumption is to assume that because it is different, it is also worse. It will help, therefore, if the visitor has at least some idea of how France works.

France is a democratic republic, headed by a President who acts through a government

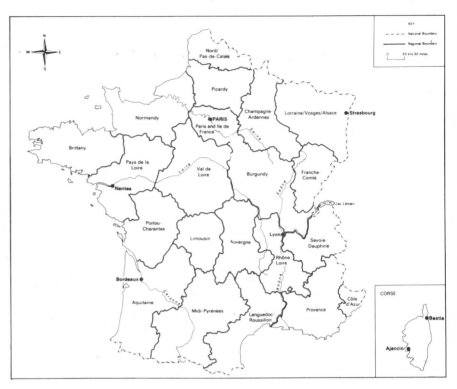

headed by a Prime Minister. The President is elected for seven years, and acts as Head of State as well as leader of the political party in power.

The Government is responsible to Parliament, a two-chamber house, consisting of a Chamber of Deputies, elected for five years, and an upper house or Senate. Senators are elected for three years on a broad franchise, and are usually senior or deputy Counsellors of State, or delegates from the larger municipalities. Most French Governments are coalitions and the present one (1984) is a Socialist grouping.

The administrative framework of France, although often changed and currently under review, is a three tier structure. The *région* or Province; the *département;* and the *municipalité* or *commune.* There are currently twenty-three regions in Metropolitan France. Some, like Normandy and Brittany are modern versions of the old countries and dukedoms of the pre-Revolutionary *Ancien Régime.* Others, like *Pays de la Loire,* are entirely modern, and quite artificial groupings. Each region contains a number of *départements,* and although this system too, is under review, the head of each *département* is the *Préfet,* who reports directly to the President of the Republic.

The *département* is the lynch-pin of the administrative structure, and the system dates back to the earliest days of the First Republic.

The twenty-three regions of France.

25

Most *départements* are named after rivers, Seine-et-Marne, Yonne, and so on. The communes or *municipalités,* are administered by a local council under a *maire,* who is elected for six years. Through this three tier system, the French people are governed, and in turn relay their wishes to the highest levels of the administration.

Services

A few notes on general services may be useful.

Time: France operates on the twenty-four hour system, so that 7.00 pm is 19.00 hours and 2.00 am is 0200 hours. France uses Summer Time and for most of the year French time is one hour ahead of Britain. This may affect your timings.

Measurements and Distance: All measurements are metric. One kilometre is approximately five-eighths of a mile, so 8km = 5 miles; 16km = 10 miles. A kilo is 2.2 lb, a litre is 1.75 pints. The Centigrade (or Celsius) system applies to temperature. The formula:

$$Temp\ °C \times 2 = X$$
$$X - (X \div 10) = Y$$
$$Y + 32 = Temp\ °F$$

is easily mastered although it looks complicated. For example:

$$16°C \times 2 = 32$$
$$32 - 3 = 29$$
$$29 + 32 = 61°F$$

Speed limits:

Auto-routes	130 km/81mph
Dual carriageways	110 km/68 mph
Single carriageways	90 km/57 mph
In Towns	60 km/40 mph
	(unless otherwise indicated)

Seatbelts are compulsory; the breathalyser *(alcool test)* is in use. All motorists must carry and use a red warning triangle if stopped by an accident, puncture or other breakdown. Traffic on a roundabout now has precedence over traffic entering it, but *priorité à droite* applies in most towns.

Banks: Banks are usually open from 0900-1200 hrs. and 1400-1700 hrs. Some open earlier and close at 1600 hrs. There are numerous public holidays and not every bank will accept travellers' cheques or exchange foreign currency. Those banks displaying the Eurocheque sign will cash U.K. bank cheques up to £50 in value if they are accompanied by a Eurocheque card. Note that this is *not* the usual U.K. cheque card, but a special *Eurocheque* card issued on application only by the High Street banks, and changed on 1st January each year.

Post Offices (Poste Téléphone Télégraphe)

PTT: Even the smallest French village will have a Post Office tucked away somewhere, and the French telephone system is excellent. To dial the U.K. the code is 19; (wait for an International line, signalled by a continuous tone), then dial 44 for the U.K. followed by the U.K. area code *minus* the initial zero, then the home number.

To phone France the code is 010 (International), then 33 (France), then the *départemental* code, and finally the subscriber's number. The *inter-départemental* code is 16. For Police, dial 17, which also connects with Mountain Rescue *(Gendarmerie Montagne),* and Ambulance. In case of fire, dial 19, for the *Sapeurs Pompiers.*

Getting to France

Getting to France is fairly easy, with nine useful ports down the Channel Coast, from Dunkerque to Santander in Spain, all giving swift access to the interior. These are Dunkerque, Calais, Boulogne, Dieppe, Le Havre, Cherbourg, St Malo, Roscoff, and Santander. This last port lies in Spain but is very close to the Western Pyrénées and served by regular Brittany Ferry crossings from Plymouth.

Many walkers will automatically travel to the hills by car or rail, using a ferry crossing, but with the current low level of charter air fares, a flight to some airport closer to the walk might be no more expensive, when all the extras for meals and accommodation are included, and will certainly save a considerable amount of time.

There are direct flights to France from many U.K. airports. Apart from Paris, they operate to Bordeaux, Montpellier, Toulouse and Perpignan (for the Pyrénées); Geneva (for the Alps); Nice, Marseille, Strasbourg, Nantes, Dijon, Lyon, Nîmes, and to Bastia and Ajaccio in Corsica. The use of air travel can save up to two days at either end of the walk which, at 15 miles a day, can mean an extra 60 miles (100km) of footpath is within your reach. It certainly pays to balance *all* the costs of getting there, by air or by ferry, then adding in the costs of rail or car travel, with whatever accommodation and subsistence costs will be incurred on the journey out and home. See how these compare and you may consider that the total cost could well justify air travel.

Ferry companies include Sally Viking, Sea-Link, P & O Ferries, Townsend-Thoresen and Brittany Ferries. Hovercraft services from Seaspeed and Hover-Lloyd are also available to Boulogne and Calais.

Airlines worth contacting include Air France, Air-Europe, Air-U.K., Dan-Air, British Airways, and Brymon. The internal French airline is Air-Inter. Schedules are subject to change, and some routes may be cut completely in the winter months.

Getting About in France

The French rail network is fast, clean, reliable, not overly expensive, and practically universal, especially if used in conjunction with the local coach services which serve even the remote country areas. To give one example, these lines are being written in the village of Les Deux Alpes in the Dauphine, reached by train to Dover, hovercraft to Boulogne, train to Paris, high speed train to Lyon, train to Grenoble, and then coach up to the village. Total journey time — 13 hours. Full details of French Rail (S.N.C.F.) services can be obtained from the French Rail offices in Piccadilly. One point worth making is that ticket controls depend on the passenger date-stamping the ticket at one of the orange *composteur* machines which stand at the entrance to every platform. Ticket inspectors travel on the trains and anyone with an 'un-composted' ticket will have to pay a heavy on-the-spot fine.

Walkers will find the rail network especially useful if it is combined with a bus trip up to the smaller villages. The bus station (*gare-routière*) is usually found next to the railway station. The only snag is that the bus network tends to operate on a *départemental* basis, so getting from one *département* to another on a bus can be difficult. Incidentally, a coach is a *car*, a car is *un auto* or *une voiture*, a shuttle bus is *une navette*.

One useful rail feature that will greatly appeal to walkers is the *trains touristique*. These are little trains, often powered by steam engines, which reach remote parts of France by little-used scenic routes. The *petit train jaune* (little yellow train) to the Cerdagne in the Pyrénées is one example, and there are others in the Alps, the Ardèche, the Basque country, and Normandy. Details can be obtained from the F.G.T.O. or the regional tourist boards.

Apart from using public transport, many walkers will choose to travel out by car, parking in a town or village, and walking on from there. There are advantages here but a word of warning too. Any car with foreign plates and a GB sticker is an easy mark for thieves. If the car has to be left, try to leave it in a garage, or the car park of an hotel, not in the street or a public place. Even in the mountains cars are not safe. On our last visit here, to walk in the Parc des Ecrins, thieves levered the hatchback window out with an ice axe, and apart from stealing all the non-walking gear, slashed the electric leads and did a lot of damage. That makes it my third

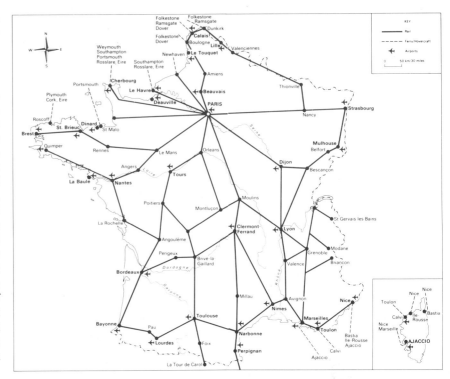

The main ferry links, principal railway lines and airports of France.

robbery in France within two years.

Clearly, nothing valuable should be left in the car, and the boot and roof-rack should be completely unloaded, even for an overnight halt. If anything is stolen the fact must be reported to the police who will note the details and provide the victim with proof of theft. Without such proof no insurance company will entertain a claim for compensation. The chances of anything being recovered are slim, so good, comprehensive and unequivocal insurance cover is clearly essential.

Cars left in mountain districts should be prepared for the extreme cold often found at high altitudes, and placed away from the possibility of flash floods or icicles falling from the eaves of buildings.

Health

Any wise walker setting out for a one-, two- or three-week journey over the hotter, higher, countryside of France will have been sensible enough to train for it beforehand and be at least fit enough to complete the average daily stage, under whatever load he or she has chosen to carry. Certainly a little pre-walk walking can be very beneficial and, as mentioned in the previous chapter, particular attention should be paid to the feet and comfortable, well broken-in footwear is essential. To the usual first-aid kit, the walker might sensibly add suncream, a lip salve, something recommended by the chemist

A walker on the GR76 near Languedoc Roussillon.

to soothe an upset stomach, and aspirin.

France has a National Health Service which operates very much on the lines of the U.K. system, with the significant difference that French patients pay for treatment and *then* reclaim all or most of the cost from the Government. Under the E.E.C. regulations British visitors are entitled to treatment but they should obtain Form E111 from the D.H.S.S. and take this with them to France. Getting the E111 involves filling in another form first, and as the whole process takes a little time it is as well to apply some weeks before the trip begins. The E111 is not available to the self-employed or the unemployed.

Most experienced walkers should be able to undertake elementary first-aid, but if something more complicated is required then French chemist shops *(pharmacies)* are obliged to give first-aid treatment and are often very good at it. Patching up a cut and bruised colleague recently, cost 14 francs. If a doctor or ambulance is required, or the party gets into real trouble on the hills, emergency services can be contacted by dialling 17.

Food

Other than on trips into very remote areas, such as across the Pyrénées, or on the GR20 in Corsica, the walker in France has no need to worry about food supplies and certainly does not need to import any food, other than some freeze-dried food for emergency use. As a rule every walk veers into a village quite often and food shops *(ravitaillement)* are indicated in the *Topo-Guides*. Such places will inevitably contain stocks of camping gas, and someone, somewhere in the village, will have petrol. Supplies of other fuels, such as meths, may be much more difficult to obtain and any walker heading for France who uses a meths or solid fuel stove should switch to one burning gas or petrol. Gas cartridges cannot be carried on aircraft and petrol containers should either be empty or very definitely leakproof.

The general shops *(alimentation)* or small supermarkets are increasingly common even in the smaller villages, but the traditional shops are still running, so that stocking up with food may involve a visit to the *boulangerie* for the bread, the *épicerie* for cheese, ham and fruit, and the *charcuterie* for the pâté and meat.

The French bread that people rave about goes stale very quickly, so it is better to buy wrapped wholemeal bread in the general store, rather than plod hopefully down the trail with several *baguettes* sticking out of the rucksack, for these will be rock-hard within hours.

Walkers on the more urban routes, or those who do not wish to cook or camp at all, will generally find cafés or a small restaurant open at convenient times, even in the smaller villages. A café will normally offer sandwiches, while the restaurants will have food which is often excellent and always inexpensive. Most offer a fixed price menu which includes the service charge, and a *carte,* which offers a wider choice. House wine usually comes in a *pichet,* a small jug.

Clothing and Equipment

Since any walk abroad involves a fairly extended trip of a week or more, the problem of what must be taken and therefore carried, is often acute. It is as well to remember that rural France is very informal. Ties and jackets are quite unnecessary, even in the most expensive and exclusive places. On the same practical level though, the walker has to remember that French walks tend to be longer, higher, hotter, or a combination of all three, and this should be borne in mind when preparing the kit list.

Any wise walker always draws up a kit list before any extended walk, and apart from the items which would be carried on a U.K. walk, thought should be given to including an ice axe, even in the summer, on any mountain walk; crampons would not be out of place from, say, October to early May on any hill route over 1970ft (600m). Other essential items are windproofs, lip-salves and face-creams; the high mountain winds will punish any face unprotected from the clear air and ultra violet rays. Colour slide film is more expensive in France, and black and white film is now almost impossible to obtain outside proper photographic shops. These will only be found in towns of some size, so adequate supplies should be taken from Britain. We suggest that one roll of colour and one of black and white per day is a good amount. Other necessary items will be the passport, a phrasebook and a pocket dictionary. These items apart, whatever the walker would normally carry on an extended walk in Britain will be perfectly adequate in France.

Having prepared a detailed kit list, the walker should make every effort to either eliminate items or carry as many items as possible on a group basis, shared out between the walkers. When venturing abroad there is an understandable temptation to take everything that might possibly come in handy, on the basis of 'Just-in-case'.

The snag with this is that it adds a great deal of unwelcome weight and bulk to the rucksack, and no walk is improved by a crushing weight on the shoulders, much of it occasioned by items which are never actually used. Cut the weight to the very minimum and concentrate only on the essential.

Planning the Walk

The purpose of these first two chapters has been to underline the two basic points that the walker who sets out to make a major walk in France will enjoy it far more if he or she has some experience of extended walking trips, which can be a very different proposition from day walking or rambles, and takes the trouble to plan the walk properly.

Secondly, the walker has to appreciate that France, especially rural France, is a very different country. Most walkers who start walking in France become addicted to it and return there again and again, delving ever deeper into the back-country. Those who try it and don't like it have, as a rule, made three cardinal errors, which have combined to spoil the experience. They have either attempted a walk beyond their competence and fitness; or they have collided headlong with the French, or both.

Before we go on to describe twenty Classic Walks in France, we beg our readers to think of these points. To get the most out of walking in France, put a little effort into the planning. Learn a little French, work out suitable daily distances, plan well ahead. Buy a copy of *Walking in France* which goes into all the points mentioned in far more detail than we have space for here. The more work that goes into the pre-planning, the more enjoyable will be the trip ... and with those points emphasised, let us begin. *En avant!*

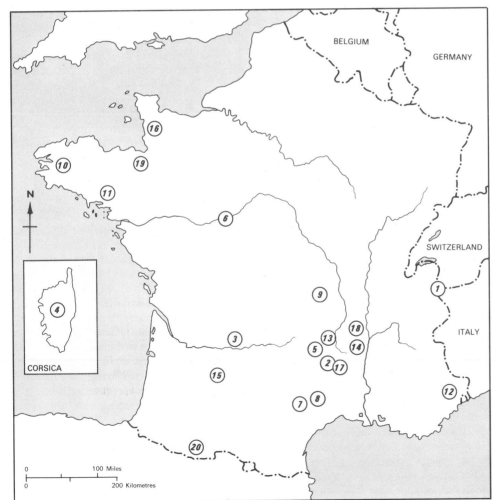

The general location of the twenty 'Classic Walks In France' selected for this book.

Walk 1 THE TOUR OF MONT BLANC

The Mer de Glace. A view of the glacier on the south slope of Mont Blanc, a good winter trip for experienced skiers.

Introduction

The Tour of Mont Blanc is certainly one of the great walks of the world. This famous footpath offers a splendid outdoor experience and a real adventure, yet it is an adventure on a human scale, a tour which any fit walker can easily complete within the span of a normal holiday. Unlike the other walks in this book, this is an international affair for the route crosses the frontiers of France, into Italy, and then into the Valais region of Switzerland before returning to the start near Chamonix.

The attraction of this walk lies principally in the scenery which is never less than spectacular, with Europe's highest mountain, Mont Blanc, 15,770ft (4807m), as the constant companion all the way round the massif. Mont Blanc in some way is the European outdoor lover's magic mountain. This is where mountain climbing, as we know it, really began. The first ascent of Mont Blanc in 1786 was organised by a Frenchman, Horace de Saussure, known as the 'Homer of Mountaineering'. He climbed it himself in the following year, and since then thousands of climbers and walkers (about ten thousand every year) have reached the top, or scrambled contentedly, as we shall do, on the lower slopes.

Terrain

The Tour does not go to the summit of the mountain. It circles the range along a number of valleys, crossing the ridges which separate them by various cols, an up-and-down route which has its southern tip at the Col de la Croix du Bonhomme in France and runs north to the Col de la Forclaz in Switzerland. The terrain is always hilly and the ascents and descents are sometimes steep but as is usual in France, the trail uses established paths, where the gradients are reasonable and takes in all the finest routes and best viewpoints, running through villages well supplied with small hotels and little cafés. Any fit walker can complete the tour comfortably inside two weeks, weather permitting.

Climate

This is high mountain country, where the weather can vary, and winter hangs on longer to the upper slopes. Be prepared for a day or two of low cloud, rain or high wind. These factors, far more than terrain, limit the walker to certain months of the year, and the full walking season is quite short, and often crowded. The high passes can be blocked with snow until mid-June, so any attempt before this requires experience with ice axe and crampons. Those walkers who always choose to carry an ice axe in the high hills are probably right to do so on the Mont Blanc Tour. The village hotels open in the spring but the *refuges* and huts are not open until the climbing season starts in mid-June, so that from the end of June to the end of July is the most convenient time for the walk, with long days, good but not too warm weather, and plenty of accommodation. August to mid-September is the holiday time, and the hills and paths are crowded. September and October are marvellous, but the nights are drawing in and the hotels are starting to close down. It is worth mentioning that when I last made the Tour, in early September, we had a heavy snowstorm above Courmayeur and continuous low cloud or rain. Maybe we were unlucky. From mid-October snowfalls can certainly be expected, and ice will be found on the higher parts of the path, even in mid-summer.

Accommodation

There is plenty of accommodation available, of all kinds, large hotels, pensions, mountain huts, climbing refuges and camp sites. Wild camping is usually permitted, although there are certain restrictions, usually inside the regional parks, and below 4920ft (1500m) in the Val d'Aosta. The problem with accommodation is linked to the time of year. This is a popular area for outdoor lovers and even the higher huts can be full with day walkers and mountain climbers.

It pays to book ahead at any time, and it is essential to do so in the high season months of July and August, or find a place to stop by mid-afternoon. At the end of the season, in early spring and late autumn, the hotels and huts are closing down so, as Chapter 2 has pointed out, a considerable degree of pre-planning is essential. A day in Chamonix or Courmayeur to make such final arrangements would be well worth while.

The path down towards Courmayeur from Monte Bianco.

31

Distance: 125 miles (200km) approximately.
Time required: Two weeks.
Type of Walk: A high mountain walk over a well-established route, requiring fitness and some hill walking experience.
Season: From mid-May to early October—see notes below.
Maps and Guides: IGN *Carte Verte* No. 45. Didier-et-Richard 1:50,000 Massif du Mont Blanc. *100 Hikes in the Alps*, Ira Spring & Harvey Edwards, (The Mountaineers). *Michelin Green Guide*. FFRP-CNSGR *Topo-Guide* (TMB) Tour du Mont Blanc.
Information: Syndicat d'Initiative, Chamonix, or Les Houches; Tourist Office, Courmayeur.
Getting There: By rail to Chamonix, or Les Houches.

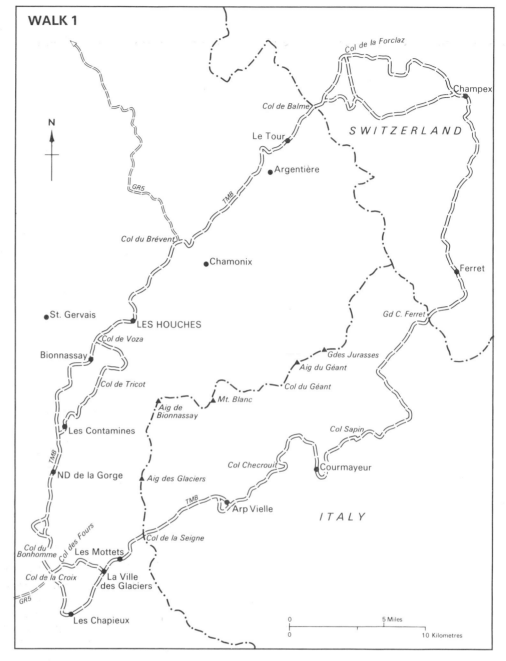

WALK 1

Equipment

The CNSGR *Topo-Guide* describes the Tour du Mont Blanc as a *randonnée-type de Moyenne montagne,* or a Grade III walk, calling for some six hours mountain walking per day, usually on paths but with some scrambling and the possibility of snow on high places. The walker will therefore require boots, warm windproof clothing for the mornings and the tops, with shorts, hat and sun-cream for the lower slopes and the warmer days. An ice axe would never look out of place, and crampons could be useful earlier or later in the year. Those who choose to camp will require full backpacking equipment, but there is plenty of accommodation so that given pre-planning, a light rucksack should be sufficient. Maps will be useful and a compass is essential for use in low cloud and mist, although the waymarking is good. Please note that different coloured waymarks are used on the TMB in Italy and Switzerland.

Conclusion

This is an exhilarating expedition for hill walkers, backpackers and keen, fit, long-distance walkers, those who love wildlife, the high mountains, and a real challenge.

The Tour

As this is a circular tour, it can be joined at any point along the route; anyone completing the circle has completed the Tour. Good access points are Champex in Switzerland, Courmayeur in the Val d'Aosta, and Chamonix in France. Although there are numerous *variantes* and even more numerous short cuts by cable car or bus, the classic Tour du Mont Blanc follows the *Topo-Guide* and begins at Les Houches, south and west of Chamonix.

Les Houches is an old and attractive mountain village with plenty of accommodation, and a helpful tourist office, a good place for walkers to sort out their equipment and get up-to-date information on the weather and accommodation situation for the days ahead. Do not leave without visiting the local museum, and if you wish, the walk can commence by taking the chairlift or train from St Gervais to the Col de Voza, two hours walk away.

From the col, and from the Mont du Prarion, 6450ft (1967m) there are splendid views over the mountains and the Chamonix valley, if you can ignore the clutter of ski lifts and mountain railway. A *variante* runs off here to the Col de Tricot, 6950ft (2120m), but our direct path descends to the old village of Bionassay, 4310ft (1314m), which has a good *gîte d'étape,* and then after about an hour, into Champel, which has a fine fountain set at the side of the hill, which we descend towards Tresse. After another three hours the TMB arrives at Les Contamines-Montjoie, a marvellous spot in which to end the first day. There is a small Nature Reserve around Les Contamines, and this medieval village has plenty of accommodation and a camp site. The tourist office has a map showing local walks, and will again up-date any information and advise on the weather for the next few days.

South of Les Contamines the TMB links up for a while with the GR5, the Holland-Mediterranean footpath, and follows the route of an old Roman road beside several rushing streams to the chalet-hotel at Nant Borrant, 4790ft (1460m), climbing gradually all the time. The views from here are spectacular, as the climb continues through the woods and open Alps to La Balon. There is a short *variante* here, but the main route goes ever upwards, over the Plan des Dames and so to the first high point on the tour,

the Col du Bonhomme, 7640ft (2329m). Those who start early will reach the col around mid-day and if the clouds and mist have disappeared, the views should be superb. To the east this col is overlooked by a double-crowned rock, called the Bonhomme and the Bonne Femme, and from here the walker can gaze south-east into the Tarantaise, or North to the Tré-la-Tête glacier. There is usually snow up here throughout the year, and it is a further short steep climb to the nearby Col de la Croix du Bonhomme, where the GR5 departs for the south and the TMB heads east, descending steadily to Les Chapieux at 5100ft (1554m). There is a *variante* of this route, over the Col des Fours, 8740ft (2665m), which, though difficult, shortens the overall route, and is far prettier, and this may appeal to walkers now well into their stride.

Les Chapieux is a good place to stock up on food, or even spend the night. This is the southern tip of the Tour and from here the country gets very wild, crossing the massif and into Italy before reaching civilization again at Courmayeur.

From Chapieux, the path climbs, on the right bank of the river, and then down to where the Col des Fours *variante* joins in at La Ville des Glaciers, a very pretty spot. From here, a great climb commences, past the *refuge* at Mottets, a wearing zig-zag slog up to the Franco-Italian frontier at the Col de la Seigne, 8250ft (2516m), a windy spot, and a significant landmark on the TMB. Here the waters divide, some to flow west into the Mediterranean, others east, towards the Adriatic. Look north to the wild cloud-capped Aiguille des Glaciers. This spot also marks the crest of the Alpine chain, dividing the French Tarantaise from the Italian Val d'Aosta. From here on, this is the *Tour del Monte Bianco,* for we have arrived in Italy.

The path across the Col de la Seigne, wild as it looks, is one of the ancient roads of history; the Romans led pack-horses over here. From this point the path descends to the green and pleasant valley that leads through the southern flank of Monte Bianco to Courmayeur. It is a full day's walk, in good conditions, from the col to Courmayeur, but since this section should not be rushed, and mountain hotels become increasingly frequent as the path descends into the Val Veni, wise walkers will either camp high, or stop as soon as possible. There are also chair lifts which cut out part of the climb from the Val Veni to the Plan Checrouit, and plenty of good, green camp sites in the valley itself.

This part of the path is fairly flat, and along the valley floor, with glaciers overhanging in the steep valleys to the north. A main path, almost

Above left: **An alternative way down from Mont Blanc if the weather turns is by cable car.**

Above right: **The Dent du Géant.**

Opposite page, above: **The Val Ferret in the foothills of Mont Blanc.**

Opposite page, below: **A cable car from Chamonix lifts you above this dramatic scenery.**

a road but also part of the TMB, runs past the Chapel of Notre Dame de la Guérison to Entreves, where the Mont Blanc tunnel emerges from the rock, and so into pretty Courmayeur, a good place to stop for a couple of days, with a helpful tourist office. Much of the route still lies ahead, but the walker should now be fit, and the daily distances will be increasing. From here, a cable car can lift you almost to the top of Mont Blanc for views to the crest and the Dent du Géant.

From Courmayeur the TMB runs north through the Val Ferret, under the spike of the Dent du Géant. The Val Ferret is one of the most beautiful parts of the walk and worth a long, lingering day. Leaving Courmayeur the walker has a choice of route, but the main path climbs up to Villair, 4350ft (1327m), and after a couple of hours arrives at the Col Sapin, 6450ft (1964m), from which there are great views north, across the Val Ferret to the high peaks of

Les Grandes Jurasses in the main massif.

From the Col Sapin the path descends to the north, and then turns east, under the Triolet glacier to Arnuva, from where another climb commences towards the next col, the Col Ferret, 8320ft (2537m), where the path runs over into Switzerland and the canton of Valais. Check the weather before departing for the col, for it is a three-hour slog and it will take a full day to reach the far side, even in good conditions. Here the waymarking changes to white-red-white bars, and yellow lozenges or arrows, or yellow and black stripes. This can be confusing but use the map and follow the main path. Glaciers predominate hereabouts, oozing down from the north. Once across the col the walker descends steadily for over 3280ft (1000m) into the village of Ferret. Wild camping is not permitted here, and the accommodation is limited, but from Ferret those with the time and energy to spare can, if the weather permits, walk up to the

heights of the Grand St Bernard.

The Swiss Val Ferret is almost as beautiful as the Italian one and the trail now is gentle, descending steadily through the woods and pastures beside the river Dranse, arriving at last at the northern point of the TMB and the village of Champex, 4810ft (1466m). Champex is an idyllic spot set beside a deep blue-green lake, with plenty of accommodation and another very helpful tourist office. Here a long *variante* swerves off the main route, to climb over the col at La Barme, a full day, to make a junction with the main trail.

Following the TMB from Champex, the walker has a full day's march to the actual northern limit of the Tour at the Col de la Forclaz, 5000ft (1526m), where there is a small and popular hotel. Fortunately there is much more accommodation available in nearby Trient. There is also a large *gîte d'étape* in the hamlet of Peuty.

There are *variantes* everywhere around here, but at Les Herbagères the long *variante* from Champex rejoins the main path which climbs to the heights of the Col de Balme, 7190ft (2191m), and so back again from Switzerland into France at another spot with marvellous views to the top of Mont Blanc and the Aiguilles Rouges.

Here again, those walkers with time to spare can take the *variante* which circles away towards Vallorcine, but the main path now runs firmly south, across the rolling shoulders or upper meadows of the alps, studded with barns on these meadows of the mountain, down to the little village of Le Tour, and so back at last into the Chamonix valley. Le Tour is a winter ski resort with plenty of hotels, and if time has run out there are buses from here to Chamonix. There are still some highlights ahead, as the path runs south past Argentière, and by the Aiguilles Rouges, which are now listed as a Nature Reserve. The footpath runs through the Reserve, up to the Chalets de Chésery, 7580ft (2005m), rising and falling along the side of the valley across Plan Praz and then a steep climb up to the last great landmark but one, the Col du Brévent, 7770ft (2368m). The views from here are magnificent and include the whole chain of the Mont Blanc massif, and the valley of Chamonix far below at the foot of the cable car. From the col an hour's stiff climb takes the walker to the top of Le Brévent, 8285ft (2526m), the high station of the cable car, for one last look at this magnificent mountain country. Then the path tilts down and down until, after two hours, the walker arrives at last, back in Les Houches and the Tour du Mont Blanc is over.

Walk 2 THE ROBERT LOUIS STEVENSON TRAIL

Introduction

Unlike the other walks in this book, the Robert Louis Stevenson Trail is not, at least for the moment, a part of the *Grande Randonnée*. The trail owes its origins to the Scots writer Robert Louis Stevenson, author of *Treasure Island* who, in the autumn of 1878, set out from Le Monastier in the Auvergne to walk south across the Cévennes accompanied by 'a small grey donkey called Modestine, the colour of a mouse, with a kindly eye'. It took this pleasing pair eleven days to complete the trip, and the book that Stevenson wrote about their journey, *Travels with a Donkey in the Cévennes*, was his first successful book and one which has since become a travel classic.

In 1978, on the centenary of Stevenson's trip, the local people, encouraged by a Scotswoman, Madame Pat Villete, decided to retrace and waymark the trail, and a group of British writers was organised by Rob Hunter to make the inaugural trip down the RLS trail on a blistering journey, which was later described by Rob as 'the biggest disaster since the Somme' ... but that's another story. Since then hundreds of British walkers have made the journey, discovering, in the process, a part of France which is very beautiful and very little changed from the way it was when Stevenson passed this way over a hundred years ago.

The walk itself is not too difficult if the weather stays cool and the walker allows sufficient time. Stevenson took eleven days, and ten would still be a comfortable allowance. The trail does cross two significant mountains, Mont Lozère, 5570ft (1699m), and Mont du Goulet, 4910ft (1497m), while the Cévennes proper, which the walker enters towards the end, are always fairly rugged terrain. The best times to make the walk are late spring, May or June, or in the autumn, between September and October. It can still be very warm and shorts will be essential. *Heavy* boots are not necessary, but *light* boots or stout trainers are essential, for the ground is frequently rough. Since summer storms and cold mornings are also possible, a fairly complete set of walking gear is advisable.

Stevenson's route can easily be followed from his book and the IGN maps. If the stages are carefully planned, and the summer months avoided, it should not be difficult to find accommodation, although this is not abundant, and

WALK 2

LE PUY
Le Monastier-Sur-Gazeille
Loire
Allier
N
Pradelles
Langogne
Notre-Dame-des-Neiges
La Bastide Puylaurent
Mt. Goulet 1497m
Le Bleymard
Mt. Lozère
Le Pont de Montvert
Tarn
Florac
St.-Germain-de-Calberte
ALÈS
St. Jean-du-Gard

0   10 Miles
0   20 Km

Distance: 120 miles (192km).
Time Required: Two weeks.
Type of Walk: A varied walk, across hilly and sometimes mountainous country; but one requiring no great experience.
Season: Spring – autumn
Maps and Guides: IGN *Carte Verte* 1:100,000, Nos. 50, 58, 59. *Travels with a Donkey in the Cévennes*, Robert Louis Stevenson (Godfrey Cave).
Getting to the start: By train and bus via Le Puy.

will vary, from good two-star hotels to the rather spartan monastery of Notre Dame des Neiges, where all true followers of Stevenson will certainly wish to stop.

Getting There

Le Monastier-sur-Gazeille is a small town, situated south-east of Le Puy and easily reached by bus and train. From the end of the walk in St Jean-du-Gard, buses run to Alès and so to Montpellier. As an introduction to France, this

The Walk

This walk begins where Stevenson's did, in the centre of the town, at a small stone obelisk by the post office, which marks his point of departure.

From here a road leads downhill to a ford across the river Gazeille, and the path leads up over the hill, and after an hour or so, down again to the infant Loire at Goudet. Have a coffee at the Hôtel de la Loire, where the owner, M. Senac, a descendant of the man who welcomed Stevenson, will show you the photograph of his ancestor the fencing master, who features in Stevenson's book. From here the path climbs up, past the ruined castle and west towards the village of Costeros on the main N88 road, which is a useful landmark. Turn back along the way and look east, towards the wild hills of the Vivarais, the modern Ardèche, to pick out Mt. Mézenc, 5750ft (1753m), and the tall cone of the Gerbier de Jonc, where the great river Loire rises.

Once across the main road the path is easy, and the faded blue and white St. Andrew's crosses of the RLS waymarking soon bring the walker into the little village of Bouchet St Nicolas. It is possible to stay here, or in the hotel by the lake which lies a little to the north. With some fifteen miles completed, this might be a good place for the first night stop.

After Le Bouchet, the walker has two easy gentle days, well worth enjoying as the trail wanders south to Landos, and on to the hilltown of Pradelles. Here in the little church you can still see the famous Virgin of Pradelles, 'which does many miracles though she be of wood'. Pradelles has clear fountains into which we once sank our burning feet, and many good little restaurants along the main street. The second stop could be made here or five miles further on at Langogne.

After Pradelles the country becomes rather more hilly as the trail passes on through Langogne, which is a sizeable place, and then into some undiscovered countryside to small villages, St. Flour-de-Mercoire and Chéylard l'Evêque, a region of field and forest, where good, close map-reading would be advisable.

Past Les Pradelles the countryside becomes very beautiful, carpeted with flowers in the spring, and here the Trail turns sharply east to come out above the Allier by the castle at Luc. Descend the hill to the village, to the point where the RLS Trail overlaps for a while with two GR routes, the GR7 and the GR4.

Our destination lies south and east, through the woods, to one of the major and most interesting stops on the Trail, the monastery of Notre-Dame-des-Neiges, Our Lady of the

A typical hill town showing the distinctive colouring and landscape of the Cévennes.

southern walk can hardly be bettered and with such a vivid, historical, and British connection, it remains the classic journey of a lifetime for British walkers.

Snows. Walking steadily, it should take the traveller about four days to get here from Le Monastier. This is the perfect spot to have a rest and prepare for the increasingly hard country that lies ahead. Stevenson spent several days in the monastery and the monks are still very hospitable. If their guest rooms are full, it is always possible to sleep in the barn; refectory meals are available and as the monks are involved in the liquor business, as many monks are, (think of Chartreuse or Benedictine) they have a well-stocked bar. Ask for the *Père Hotelier* on arrival or when phoning ahead.

After the stop at Notre-Dame-des-Neiges, the traveller turns west again, following the path down to La Bastide-Puylaurent, and then on to Chassarades, about eight miles away, where the first real climbs of this journey begin. Cross the little river Chassezac and set out for the crest of La Goulet 4910ft (1497m), via the little village of Lestampes. This is a stiff ascent through the woods, but once on the crest the path falls away and there is a fairly easy descent down the south side of the mountain to the village of Le Bleymard.

Le Bleymard is a ski resort in its own small way, which gives an indication that the winters hereabouts can be both long and hard. Ahead lies the mountain where the skiing takes place, Mont Lozère, 5570ft (1699m), a very fine peak where the slopes are still not completely marred, even by the odd ski lift.

Here again, the path is due south and not difficult to follow. The view from the top, by the col de Finiels, is well worth the effort. On a clear cold spring day one can look south and glimpse the distant Mediterranean, while all around lie the rolling hills of the Cévennes, a vast, scantily populated region, one of the most attractive and unspoilt parts of France, once the refuge of the

The ruined castle at Goudet which is seen on the first day's walk.

One of the seven branches of the Gardon river.

Camisards. These were Huguenot refugees who refused to leave France after the Revocation of the Edict of Nantes by Louis XIV, and they fought a guerrilla war hereabouts for over a hundred years, up to the time of the Revolution. The small abandoned farms, even empty villages, which the walker will encounter on the way, are an echo of that long struggle.

From the col de Finiels the best way down to the next staging point, Le Pont de Montvert on the Tarn, is by the D20 road, since the fields are heavily fenced. Le Pont de Montvert is a pretty spot, and the journey here from Notre-Dame-des Neiges should be a very pleasant, if tough, two-day march.

At Le Pont de Montvert, the walker has a problem. Stevenson followed a track west for twenty kilometres, to Florac, but this track is now a main road, often occupied by heavy lorries. The best way today is to cross the river at Montvert and follow the minor road uphill for a while before striking west on a forest trail, using map and compass, and descending before Florac into the valley of the Mimente on any one of a number of forest paths. This section can take the best part of a day, and a further night stop in Florac, a pleasant spot full of hotels, will refresh the walker for the next stage, a full day into the very heart of the Cévennes.

The best way out of Florac, and close to the one followed by Stevenson, is up the bed of the old railway line which follows the course of the Mimente. The rails have long gone but the tunnels and bridges still remain, though these bridges are a little creaky. Kick the path hard

and the rotting wood of the railway sleepers just below the surface will spout splinters beneath your feet. This path is well graded and fairly easy all the way up the river valley, and it eventually crosses to the south side by Cassagnas. It is possible to press on up this valley to a well-known walker's viewpoint at the Col de Jalcrest but, by the remains of an old signal box on the railway, our path veers sharply south, up the hillside, and commences a climb for the crest. There, according to Stevenson, the traveller arrives at a watershed. Behind, all the rivers flow eventually into the Garonne and so to the Atlantic. From now on they will flow south for the not-far-distant Mediterranean and here, as I recall, we too felt that sudden change, that warm, scented air with the peculiar meridional tang of dwarf oak and tar, the *garrigue*, a definite touch of the blushful south — delightful.

It is a steep twisting scramble down the hillside to the Arab horse stud at La Serre de la Cam. Apart from being a stud farm there is also a *gîte d'étape*, with very comfortable rooms where those who have marched this far from Florac will be very glad to spend the night, and a good restaurant. More accommodation is available further down the valley, in St-Germain-de-Calberte.

The end of the journey is almost in sight, but it is better to linger in such delightful country and take two days for the final leg of the trip, a gentle stroll down the valley through St Etienne-Vallée-Française where, just after the river bridge, the path turns off the road and ascends for the last climb, and then down again, a wide stony path through the woods to the last valley, and the end of the Stevenson's journey, at St-Jean-du-Gard.

This journey has no official *Topo-Guide* but the route is easy to follow using a copy of *Travels with a Donkey* and a good 1:100,000 map. The *Syndicat d'Initiative* at Le Monastier used to produce an English/French guidebook, which may still be available. In the years since we walked it though, many more British travellers have wandered in the footsteps of Stevenson and it is reasonable to hope that the Trail is now quite distinct and therefore easy to follow.

The castle at Arlempdes which is close to Le Monastier and worth a visit in the evening.

Walk 3 THE ROAD TO ROCAMADOUR

Introduction

This fairly short and not very difficult walk is included here for a number of reasons. Firstly, the country it covers between Brive and Vers is very beautiful and little explored by the rambler. Secondly, it will take the walker to a number of splendid places and is a careful balance of fine countryside, such as the *petits causses* (plateaux) of the Causse de Gramat and the Causse de Martel, and some exquisite little towns, Marcillac, Turenne, Martel, and above all, Rocamadour, the fantastical pilgrimage town of France which clings to the cliffside of a fissure created by the river Alzou. Rocamadour claims to be the second most beautiful place in France, ceding the first title to Mont St Michel, but for my money, Rocamadour is much more striking.

This short section of the much longer GR46 trail is also known as the *'Sentier Edmond Michelet'* after the gentleman who made an annual pilgrimage with his family from Marcillac to Rocamadour, rather as Charles Péguy used to do from Notre Dame to Chartres.

The walker with the time available can continue down the GR46/36 into the valley of the Aveyron, to such pretty places as St Antonin-Noble-Val and Penne, but even those who restrict themselves to this section of the footpath will certainly enjoy an addictive taste of what walking in France has to offer.

The pilgrim town of Rocamadour which 'clings and climbs up the side of the gorge'.

Getting There

Getting to Brive is best accomplished by train and will take a full day from the Channel coast, and as much to get home again from Cahors. Many of the towns on the way are places to linger in; Martel and Rocamadour are worth a full day of any walker's time, so those who decide to allow two weeks for the complete journey are probably wise.

It is recommended that the high season months of July and August be avoided. The weather can be very hot and, as this is a popular touring area for car-borne travellers, the crowds in the towns are considerable and accommodation can be very hard to find.

Out of high season, there is plenty of accommodation and the walker can go lightly equipped. Shorts, suncream and light boots or stout trainers are the only essential items.

The Route

This path begins in the busy, attractive little town of Brive-la-Gaillarde, in the *département* of the Corrèze. Brive is a bustling place, full of hotels and restaurants, on the direct rail line from Paris. It's an old town where the inner 'bourg' behind the encircling *boulevards* is worth exploring, a district full of old houses, alleyways and containing, as a central gem, the Church of St Martin.

The real start of this walk though is at Marcillac, a scattered village 4 miles (7km) away to the south-west, and it is from the Chapel of Our Lady in Marcillac that the trail begins.

From the Chapel the path runs south, following a very minor road that winds to the east, to the crossroads at Mont Plaisir, where a footpath turns south, along a valley to Jugeals-Nazareth, and then across more open country to the hilltop town of Turenne. The tall tower which dominates the town here, the Tour de César, has nothing to do with Julius, but this was the home of Henri-de-la-Tour-d'Auvergne, Vicomte de Turenne, Marshal of France to Louis XIV. He received the viscountcy for his services, an honour the family finances were unable to sustain and the estate was eventually sold back to Louis XV. Most of Turenne predates the eighteenth century, and the town is much more reminiscent of the Middle Ages when the great Tower was built. Turenne is a pretty spot, with great views from the old walls, and at least one good restaurant.

Leave Turenne by the little road for La Gironie, turning off to the south just after this little hamlet, and taking the footpath that leads to Les Terres Basses. This countryside is very

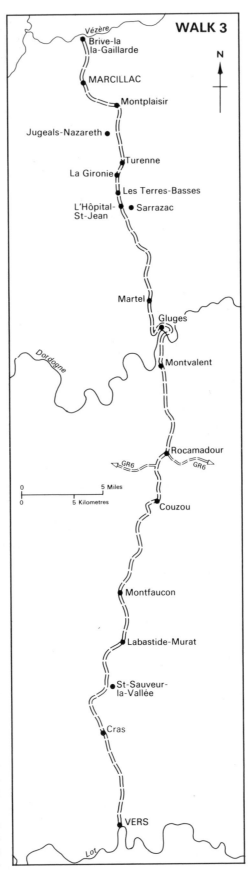

WALK 3

N

Vézère
Brive-la-Gaillarde
MARCILLAC
Montplaisir
Jugeals-Nazareth
Turenne
La Gironie
Les Terres-Basses
L'Hôpital-St-Jean   Sarrazac
Martel
Gluges
Montvalent
Dordogne
Rocamadour
GR6   GR6
0   5 Miles
0   5 Kilometres
Couzou
Montfaucon
Labastide-Murat
St-Sauveur-la-Vallée
Cras
VERS
Lot

Distance: 65 miles (109km).
Time required: One week.
Type of walk: A pleasant, interesting hill walk across the hill country of Corrèze and the plateau of Quercy.
Season: Spring or autumn.
Maps and Guides: FFPR-CNSGR *Topo-Guide* GR46. IGN *Carte Verte* 1:100,000 Nos. 57 and 64.
Getting to the Start: Train to Brive-la-Gaillarde via Paris.

Above: **Directly above a campsite is the abbey of Rocamadour from which this spectacular view of the River Alzou can be seen.**

Opposite page, top: **The open windy country of the Causse de Martel in high summer.**

Opposite page middle: **The castle at Beynac on the Dordogne, viewed from the nearby campsite. The river offers an ideal spot for a refreshing swim.**

Opposite page, bottom: **A distant view of Rocamadour bathed in early morning light.**

agreeable, fairly rolling, a mixture of orchard and pasture, divided by low stone walls, and although the gradient is gentle, the land is rising steadily up to the windy open country of the Causse de Martel.

A *causse* is a plateau and these high windswept tablelands, south of Brive, are the *petits causses*, overshadowed in size by the higher and more desolate Moyens and Grands Causses which lie further to the south-east. The sparse grasslands of the *causse* are used as sheep pasture and flocks will be wandering everywhere, accompanied by a jangle of bells.

Before the *causse*, the path reaches the village of L'Hôpital-St-Jean near Sarrazac. This was built to shelter lepers in the twelfth century by an early Viscount of Turenne, and later passed to the care of the Knights Hospitaller who looked after the sick, and guarded pilgrims who were on the road to Rocamadour, as part of their pilgrimage to Compostela in Spain. The land here hovers at the 1970-2300ft (600-700m) mark, and the path crosses the little river Doue, then through a farm and descends into the town

of Martel.

As towns go, Martel is barely a village, with less than two thousand inhabitants, but it's an ancient place. The town arms bear the blazonry of Charles Martel who defeated the Saracens at Poitiers in the eighth century, which was long before the days of blazonry, but let that pass; Martel is a little gem. The old open hall in the tiny central square is still used for weekday markets; other fine buildings include the old mint, the Hôtel de la Monnaie, the Church of St Maur, which is fortified, and the Maison Fabbri,

One of the many *Quercyçois* dovecotes that can be seen in this region of France.

St Cirq-Lapopie.

which is now the Syndicat d'Initiative.

It was in the Maison Fabbri, in 1183, that Henry Fitzhenry, son of Henry II of England, died in misery. He had robbed the nearby shrine at Rocamadour some days previously and his untimely and sudden death was regarded as God's just vengeance. Martel is a fine place to spend a day and worth such an extended stop before taking up the trail again across the highlands of Quercy.

Quercy is an ancient county of France, lying to the east of the more populated Dordogne; and noted for dovecotes and a remarkable dark wine, the *vin de Cahors*. This, the 'black wine of Quercy' was held to be so good that it spurred the Plantagenet rulers of Aquitaine into constant invasions, and until the Russian Revolution of 1917, it was the approved communion wine of the Russian Orthodox Church. From now on, every meal and picnic will be incomplete without a bottle of the *'bon Cahors'*.

Leaving Martel, the path proceeds south and climbing slightly arrives at the crest of the Causse de Martel, overlooking the deep green valley of the Dordogne at Gluges. Gluges has a fine little Romanesque church, and marvellous views over the winding river far below. From here the path winds down the side of the valley to the river itself, and over the iron bridge that spans it, at Montvalent. Montvalent is a little tourist centre, with small hotels, camp sites and restaurants, and yet another pilgrim stop on the Compostela *variante*.

Crossing the Dordogne valley, the walker climbs again, up from the green valley to the golden expanses of the *causse,* and on past various *montjoies,* or small hills, which give glorious views south towards Rocamadour, tucked away out of sight, past the Pilgrim's Cross by Alis, and out to yet another escarpment which looks across the steep, deep valley of the river Alzou, to the pilgrim town of Rocamadour, a stunning sight.

Rocamadour is a marvel. It clings and climbs up the side of the gorge, a beautiful and amazing sight. One can't imagine anyone building a town like that today, more's the pity. The origins of Rocamadour are obscure but the story goes that this was once the home of St Amadour, an Anchorite monk. His relics were discovered in the eighth century, and a shrine was built to contain them, a shrine which eventually obtained one of the rare Black Virgins, Notre Dame de Rocamadour. Our Lady of Rocamadour, patron of soldiers, cares for military men. Knights swore their vows before Our Lady of Rocamadour, and it was her reputation as a patron of soldiers which led Henry Fitzhenry to pillage her shrine and take the

treasure to pay his mercenaries, as well as the sword Durandel, which had once belonged to Roland the Paladin. Although all this has gone, the Virgin of Rocamadour is still there, in that smoky little chapel in the rocks, her eyes still fixed hopefully on the door. Apart from this charming chapel, hung with votive offerings, Rocamadour is best viewed from the facing escarpment. Close to, it's a tourist trap, especially in summer when the streets and hotels are jammed with visitors. Go there a little out of season and see it at its best.

Leave Rocamadour by the lower gate, and follow the river south, to the little stone bridge which marks the place where the GR46 and the GR6 (Alpes-Océan) meet. The Alzou valley is very attractive, a green, cool spot below the cliffs of the *causse*. From here the route is a mixture of footpath, farm track and commune road, leading the way down to the next major landmark, Couzou. Couzou was noted hereabouts for cheese, the *Cabecou*, a product of the goats which roam the *causse*. It can still be obtained for a picnic lunch before passing on to the little *bastide* of Montfaucon, perched on a low hill.

A *bastide* is a fortified town. *Bastides* were built in the thirteenth century by the French and English lords of Quercy and the Dordogne to stake their claims to this disputed frontier zone. As *bastides* go, Montfaucon is a small one, but still very attractive, and the strong town of this southern *causse,* the Causse de Gramat.

Four miles (6 km) further across the *causse,* lies another now historic spot, Labastide-Murat, which was unremarkable until the end of the eighteenth century when it became the birthplace of Joaquin Murat, who commanded the cavalry of the Emperor Napoleon. Murat's parents kept the local inn, humble enough beginnings for a man who became first a Marshal of France and then (for a brief period) King of Naples, before being deposed and shot by his unloving subjects. The full story of Murat's dramatic life is displayed in his former home, which is now a museum.

After Labastide-Murat, the path descends, past St Sauveur-la-Vallée in a network of small hills and valleys, and then past Cras, along the valley of the Vers and at last, after a further 15 miles (24km) into Vers itself, at the point where that little stream runs into the river Lot.

This walk is ideal for those travellers in France who have a few days to spare, or those walkers who enjoy a journey which takes them to historic and beautiful places by quiet footpaths — a classic combination in itself.

Walk 4 THE CORSICAN HIGH ROUTE

Introduction

It has to be stressed that the GR20, the Corsican *Haute Route,* is not an easy route. It is all too easy to imagine that any walk of only 120 miles (200 km) across an island situated in the Mediterranean, just south of the sun-kissed Riviera, must be a delightful stroll, but in Corsica at least, this would be a considerable error.

Some combination of climate and terrain links here to create a walk which can easily turn out to be exceptionally severe. The local Tourist Board asked us to stress this point, so be aware of the difficulties you may encounter, at the planning stage, and take them into account.

Corsica is a remarkably beautiful and remarkably rugged island. Even in a car, it is possible to stop on one hill and see a village just across the valley, which seems close enough to touch in that clear air, and then spend several hours driving down to the valley floor and up again, before you actually reach it. The GR20 is never level and the climbs and descents are quite relentless, so it will help to be *very* fit at the start, and resigned to extremes of weather.

The climate varies. It is a shock to arrive on the island in June and find snow on the tops, and one or two ski lifts still in operation — yes, you can ski in Corsica, both downhill and cross-country, for about seven months of the year in some places.

Even in high summer, the high central peaks attract mist, violent electrical storms, hail, and searing heat. At night the temperature can fall to well below zero. Those walkers who seek a real challenge are almost sure to find it in Corsica.

The GR20 follows the high watershed of the central mountains which span the island from north-west to south-east, between Calenzana, which lies close to Calvi, and Conca in the south, close to Porto Vecchio. On the way it

Distance: 120 miles (200km).
Time Required: Three weeks.
Type of Walk: A high mountain walk requiring considerable experience and fitness. This is not a journey to be undertaken lightly and considerable planning and preparation is advisable.
Season: Late spring to early autumn.
Maps and Guides: FFRP-CNSGR *Topo-Guide* GR20, *Sentier de La Corse.* IGN 1:100,000 Nos. 73 and 74.
Getting to the Start: By air to Ajaccio or Bastia and train to Calvi.

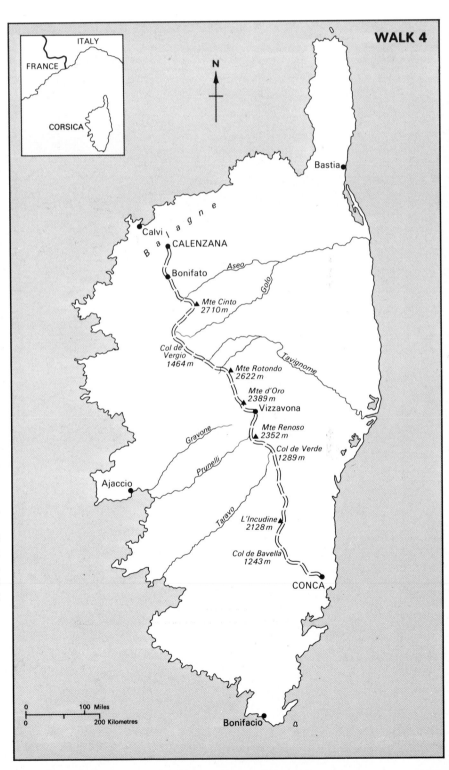

runs over high peaks like Monte Rotondo, 8600ft (2622m), Monte d'Oro, 7715ft (2352m), and the Col de Verde, 4230ft (1289m). Water and the chance to stock up with food can be in short supply, and so this trip calls for the full backpacking equipment, with ice axe, and even crampons would not be out of place before the end of June. I have seen people on snowshoes near Vizzavona in May.

The best time to make the journey would be some time between mid-June and early September, but this is high mountain country, and one cannot be dogmatic about this. The terrain is demanding and the CNSGR recommend that even those experienced and fit enough for the trip should allow a full fifteen days for the actual walk, so we recommend a three-week trip, with time to get there and adjust to the climate at the start, and have a rest on the beach after the journey is complete. As a final point, fire is an ever-present risk here in summer, so fires are forbidden, smoking strongly discouraged, and great care should be taken with stoves anywhere outside a village. Accommodation, where it exists, consists of small *refuges,* and in summer these can be crowded, so it is better to camp. These mountains are sparsely inhabited, and so the opportunities to re-stock with food are very limited everywhere and non-existent between Vergio and Vizzavona and between the Col de Verde and Bavella. Wise walkers will plan this journey in small groups and carry up to five days food, including plenty of AFD lightweight rations imported from the U.K.

It is fair to add that, especially in a book which takes time to research, write, edit, print and publish, any information is subject to change. The facts given here were correct as at September 1983 and if anything, the services and facilities should improve as time passes — but don't rely on it.

The Walk

Corsica is a beautiful island, where the air is heavy with the smell of the *maquis,* that close-knit covering of wild flowers, gorse, pine and oak scrub, loud with the buzz of bees and the chirrup of grasshoppers.

The GR20 begins on the south-east of Calenzana, a village at a modest 900ft (275m), with good views to the hills which lie ahead. The path runs up directly, climbing steadily through the trees to the first plateau for a small breather before tackling the ridge that dominates the Melaghia valley, which is usually filled with a rushing torrent — so far, so pleasant. The path crosses the river, passes the forester's hut at Bonifato, and crosses and re-crosses the river up

to the heights called Spasimata at 3905ft (1190m). This torrent should be crossed with some care if the waters are high. There are swaybridges, but they are often washed away, and some wading or rock-hopping may be necessary. Continue climbing to the high point and the little lake at Muvrella, which makes a good camping place. To get here can take a full and tiring day, but it will give a fair taste of what is to follow. If the evening is clear, try the small

Opposite page top: **A rare flat path through the thick forests of Corsica.**

Opposite page bottom: **The rough terrain in the high mountains of Corsica can be hard going.**

Above: **The dry, arid conditions and sparse population of Corsica mean it is essential to carry sufficient water and food.**

49

The hill town of Zonza on the Haute Route.

variante that leads east up to the top of the Muvrella ridge at 7045ft (2148m).

Next day the path continues to the south along the ridge, past the ski station of Haut Asco, where there is a small hotel — but don't rely on its being open. This lies 1640ft (500m) below and to the east of the ridge and can also be reached by a *variante,* although the round trip will take half-a-day.

Walkers in Corsica get to dread losing height, so follow the ridge, climbing steadily to the Punta Culaghia, descending to the higher slopes of the Asco valley. Monte Cinto, 8888ft (2710m), the highest peak hereabouts, overlooks this valley from the east and is a good landmark.

From the Asco valley the path contours round to the head of the valley and then climbs a little to the *refuge* of Altore, on the north slope of the Col Perdu, which as the name implies is a desolate spot set at around 6560ft (2000m). The nights up here can be very cold indeed, so

that good arctic sleeping bags will be useful.

This might be another good place to stop and rest, for the next section of the walk, the traverse of the Cirque de la Solitude, is said to be the hardest of the entire walk, and the walker will probably now feel tired and not yet fit enough. The scenery is certainly very impressive, and the frequent descents and ascents steep and 'airy'. Beware of stonefalls. Cable hand-holds have been strung across the more exposed parts of the peak, but it is as well to take this section carefully and not rely on them. The path dips sharply from the Col Perdu to the bottom of the Cirque, then climbs equally steeply to the Bocca Minuta, at 7275ft (2218m), a gasping ascent. There is no relief there though, for the path falls away directly for some 2625ft (800m), levels out briefly, then climbs again to the next col, the Col de Foggiale and the Refuge des Mori at 6560ft (2000m). This slog will take all day and leave even the fit walker well spent. Luckily this *refuge* is well equipped and being so remote, is rarely crowded.

From here the path swings west for a while, contouring the mountain, to the meadows and sheepfolds south of Tula, and then it picks up a *draille* or drove-road, following this down the left bank of the Golo torrent to a waterfall and into the Valdoniello forest. Here it arrives at a metalled road serving the ski station at Castel di Vergio, where there is a small hotel. After several days in the hills, this firm, smooth road is bliss beneath the feet.

This road, the D84, is a welcome sight after days on mountain paths, and depending on the date of your journey, it *should* be possible to restock with provisions at the shop by the hotel, and even have a meal there before returning to the Col de Vergio and setting out for Vizzavona, the next major landmark on the route. As a bonus, the start of the trail through the forest is marvellously flat, at least as far as the Col St Pierre, where the climbing begins again, to Bocca Redda and the gentler landscapes near the Lac de Nino, a region of meadows and shady trees. A little way past the Lac de Nino, another path veers off to the hill town of Corte. Those who have had enough or have no more time left, can follow this path into Corte, a very attractive town, and pick up a train there for Bastia or Ajaccio.

The countryside hereabouts is perceptibly gentler than that north of the Col de St Pierre, and the path contours the hillsides fairly easily to the *refuge* at Manganu, but then it again becomes progressively more rugged, following a ridge to the Bocca Soglia, at 6730ft (2052m), and the lake at Rinoso, from which a further climb takes the walker up to one of the great viewpoints on the route, the Col de la Haute Route 7235ft (2206m), a long ridge and a major watershed. From here, probably after a long pause, the walker will descend to the *refuge* at Pietra-Piana, 6040ft (1842m), on a very stony, fairly flat plateau. This, too, is a beautiful, spot, overlooked by Monte Rotondo 8600ft (2622m) to the north, and the centre for a small network of footpaths including one major *variante* off the GR20. If the weather is clear, and it may not be clear for long, a good half-day's walk will take the walker to the top of the Rotondo and back.

Following the main GR trail, the path leads south and west to the Refuge de l'Onda and then south along the ridge to the west of the Monte d'Oro, through the Bocca di Fumerella, by the Cascade des Anglais and so down, wearily, into Vizzavona, which is a little over half way, and the lowest point, at a mere 3020ft (920m), in terms of altitude, on the entire course of the walk.

Vizzavona is quite a large town, with shops, a post office, several hotels and, for those who have had enough of the hills, good connections home via Ajaccio and Bastia. A day's rest would be a good idea before passing on to the finish.

Leaving Vizzavona, the path climbs through the forest. Personally, once fit, I find climbing less wearing and far easier on the toes than descending and the climb is at least gradual, with zig-zags up to the Col de Palmente, 5395ft (1645m), where the path crosses the ridge and contours down the far slope to the Crête de Chufindu, where there is a small ski station and a *refuge*.

The path follows the ski-station service road for a while, past the hump of Monte Renoso, and then heads south across rolling country, with plenty of shade, to the forested plateau of Gialgone at 4560ft (1390m), where the path turns east, first to the Col de la Flasca, and carries on east either on or just south of the main ridge, to the Col de Verde, 4230ft (1289m), which is a crossing point for another metalled road, the D69. This section, from Vizzavona to the Col de Verde, is very pleasant, not too steep and, as any walker who has made it this far will be very fit, it can be accomplished in good time, though two days would make for pleasant walking.

As is usual in Corsica, that relentless island, the rolling, pleasant country doesn't last for long. After the Col de Verde the path climbs up and up to Punta Capella at 6560ft (2000m). The rocks here are strewn across the path and make for hard going, but then the path descends for a

The magnificent ramparts of Bonifacio.

Above: **Getting fit on a day's walk in Corsica before setting out on the three-week walk.**

Top right: **The ports of Corsica are popular with fishermen and yachtsmen alike.**

Right: **The rugged volcanic peaks of Corsica that create the conditions for strenuous walking.**

while to the open Col de Rapari, 5295ft (1614m), and then down a little more to the Col de Laparo at 5000ft (1525m). After this point though, the climbing begins anew as the path zig-zags up the hillsides to the Punta Mozza at 5905ft (1800m), and the open stony hillsides of the Monte Formicola, from which the path descends to the *refuge* at Usciolu. Water can be very scarce on this section, so carry plenty with you in spite of the weight.

From Usciolu the path follows the ridge south and west to the ridge at Lattone, climbing above the treeline and with views to the sea now in sight to the west. The rock formations here are wind-eroded and very striking. The path continues south, through empty country, over the swingbridge and so to the Pedinielli *refuge* on the right bank of the Casamintellu brook.

The path runs due east for a while up to the ridge of Foce Aperta, past the Col de Luana, where it turns sharply right and follows the ridge south to the Incudine at 6970ft (2124m), then down a gulley, or *couloir,* to Asinao at the foot of the valley. From the bottom the path winds up the steep slope to the *refuge* which is in sight on the hillside above. Once at the *refuge* the walker can see the high and jumbled rocks around the Col de Bavella, the last major barrier on the walk. The path climbs towards the col, and then across a vast grassy reach up to the final ridge.

To be honest, there *are* other ridges on this last section of the walk, but each is a little lower than the last as the land falls away, the path descending like a stairway through the trees, until it arrives at the hill above Conca, and then out on to the road at last, and so into the village and the end of this hard but memorable journey.

The GR20 rates as a Classic Walk partly because it is probably the toughest walk in France, and partly because it takes the traveller into the remotest parts of an otherwise crowded and very popular resort island. This walk calls for experience, common sense and tenacity.

Walk 5 THE GR65: THE ROAD TO COMPOSTELA

Introduction

The Road to Compostela is one of the great journeys of history. This pilgrim path to the shrine of St James in Spanish Galicia was pioneered by a Bishop of Le Puy in the tenth century and still flourishes today, a route that takes pilgrims across France and the Pyrénées into Spain, to the 'good city of the Apostle', Santiago de Compostela. There were, and still are, four 'roads' to Compostela, from Paris, Vezelay, Arles and Le Puy, but the route from Le Puy is the most important, the most scenically beautiful, the most interesting historically, and probably the most ancient. A Bishop of Le Puy is numbered among one of the earliest pilgrims and with the establishment of

the GR65 *Chemin de St Jacques de Compostelle* footpath, which retraces much of the old footpath from Le Puy to the Pyrénées, a flavour of the past can be easily recaptured. There are in fact five *Topo-Guides* describing the GR65 between Le Puy and the Spanish frontier. The total distance would be a considerable walk, and still leave the traveller with more than 500 miles (800km) to go before arriving in Compostela. Therefore, for this book we have chosen to begin at the beginning, by the Cathedral in Le Puy, and finish at the great church of Ste Foy in the hill-town of Conques, one of the most beautiful hill-towns of France. Allowing time to get out and home again, this

The abbey at Conques on the road to Compostela.

WALK 5

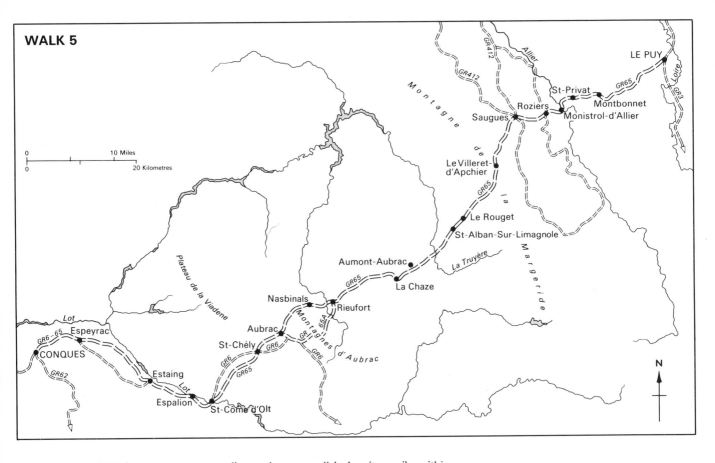

Distance: 140 miles (226km).
Time Required: Two weeks.
Type of Walk: A varied long-distance walk across moderate terrain, suitable for long-distance walkers and lightly-equipped backpackers.
Season: Late spring to October.
Maps and Guides: FFPR *Topo Guide* GR65 *Chemin de St Jacques de Compostelle* (Le Puy to Conques). *The Pilgrimage to Compostella,* Edwin Mullins (Secker & Warburg). *The Road to Santiago,* Walter Starkie (John Murray). *The Road to Compostela,* Rob Neillands (Moorland Publishing Co.).
Getting to the Start: Air to Lyon, then train to Le Puy.

walk can be accomplished quite easily within two weeks, and it takes in some marvellous places, the plateau of the Aubrac, the valley of the Lot, the green hills of the Aveyron. Those who wish to pass on to Cahors and across the Gers to the distant Pyrénées, or even to Compostela, will already be well on their way, and the rest of the journey can, and should, be completed on another occasion.

The terrain presents no real difficulties and the weather, except in high summer, should not be too hot. Snow can lie on the desolate Aubrac plateau, which lies at the 3280ft (1000m) mark, until early April, and the summer walker should be prepared for cool days and even the odd downpour. There is plenty of accommodation in hotels, *gîtes d'étape,* or on camp sites. The Compostela pilgrim, wearing a scallop shell, the *Coquille de St Jacques,* which marks his or her purpose, will be welcome everywhere.

The wise walker will begin this journey by reading one or more of the books listed in the bibliography, for the Road to Compostella is no ordinary journey. It is a piece of living history, a fragment of the past. Those who make this journey today are part of a continuum which has lasted for at least a thousand years, and looks well set for a thousand more. Lovers of history and travel will find here a combination

The abbey at Marcillac.

of both delights, and knowing the background to the journey will add greatly to their enjoyment.

The Route

The journey begins in the great city of Le Puy on the Loire, which is well worth exploring. The climb to the little chapel of St Michel de l'Aiguille, St Michael of the Needle, set on a high spike of rock, will be quite memorable. The footpath leads out of the city by the rue St Jacques and the rue de Compostela onto the high ground which offers the departing pilgrim a last view of the city before climbing up to around the 328ft (100m) mark, and heading west across the hills of the Velay to La Roche and Montbonnet, where the St Roch Chapel is a pilgrim halt, and so after a scramble down the hillside into St-Privat, on the river Allier, a tributary of the Loire, which is a good place to stop on the first day, after six hours or so of walking. St-Privat has plenty of accommodation, including a large *gîte d'étape.*

From St-Privat the pilgrim path passes on to Monistrol, 3 miles (5km) further on, another good place to stop, 16 miles (26km) from Le Puy. The village is set in a deep valley by the river, and the Hotel Sarda is run by a Welshman and his French wife, who are always pleased to see British walkers. The church carries carvings made down the centuries by travellers to Compostela.

At Monistrol the pilgrim trail crosses the Allier and passes from the Velay, the country around Le Puy, into the Gevaudan, a wilder part of France. After Monistrol the path climbs sharply towards Montaure, 3350ft (1022m), following the exact course of the medieval trail, crossing the Allier again and following the Road to Saugues, past the Chapel of La Madeleine, and so to Escluzels, through marvellous hilly country with Montaure to the north, and so after a couple of hours to Roziers and Vernet. The height along this part of the trail hovers around the 3280ft (1000m) mark, and there can be snow up here in the late spring.

From Vernet, a short walk brings the traveller to Saugues, a fairly substantial little place, with a *gîte d'étape,* several hotels and shops, a fine church and the medieval Tour des Anglais. Saugues was one of the gathering points for the medieval pilgrimage, where those from the northern Auvergne joined those coming from Le Puy. It was hereabouts, in the eighteenth century, that the fabulous Beast of the Gevaudan was said to roam, a monster wolf, or even werewolf, which was finally killed by the King's huntsmen, who shot it with a silver bullet. Saugues is another pleasant stop and a good place to spend the night.

From Saugues the pilgrim passes on through rugged country to La Clauze, a very fine little village, and then on past Le Villeret-d'Apchier, across rolling countryside to the village of La Chapelle-de-l'Hospitalet-du-Sauvage, built for

Top: **The pilgrim bridge out of Conques.**

Above: **The gentle slopes of the Aubrac can offer easy walking so long as the weather isn't too extreme – for then the lack of shelter or windbreaks can make it tough.**

Above: **The Aubrac in winter. A *gîte*** **offers welcome shelter after a day's skiing. Snow can lie here until early April.**

Right: **The medieval town of Aubrac set in the desolate plateau.**

the pilgrim traffic in the twelfth century by the Knights Templar, and maintained after their extirpation in 1314 by the Knights of St John. The present chapel is dedicated to St Roch.

From here, at the 4265ft (1300m) mark, the path descends and follows the valley of the Limagnole, through Le Rouget, a pretty spot, and after another hour, past a castle and into St Alban-sur-Limagnole, an agreeable little town in the shade of the Margeride plateau and named,

most happily, for St Alban, England's proto-martyr. The path from here runs across the granite country of the Margeride, and is very beautiful. A good morning's walk will take the traveller across the river Truyère at Les Estrets and down to the little town of Aumont-Aubrac.

Aumont is a fine little town at the north-eastern side of the Aubrac plateau, one of those delightful, undiscovered parts of France, which those who know it prefer to keep secret. In the

Top left: **The three waymark signs indicate 1.** *Gîte d'étape* **on the GR65. 2. That it should take about 2 hours 15 minutes to reach St Chély d'Aubrac. 3. It should take about 2 hours 30 minutes to reach Nasbinals.**

Bottom left: **The tympanum on the west door of the abbey at Conques.**

Above: **The pilgrim road across the Aubrac.**

spring, after the snow melts, this is a place of deep pools, rushing streams, a carpet of wild flowers, and is quite beautiful. It is also very desolate, virtually treeless and empty of people.

Leaving Aumont, follow the trail out to the west, to La Chase-de-Pyre, and past the little Chapel of the Bastide, on the D987. So far this is easy walking, over pleasant country, picking up minor roads here and there, through Lasbros and then a long section, 19 miles (29km) to the next major stopping place, Aubrac, in the centre of the plateau.

Those who camp can break their journey here easily, and Nasbinals has plenty of accommodation available, and is an old stop on the Pilgrim Way. The road to Nasbinals leads through the ruined farm houses at Rieutort d'Aubrac, at 3895ft (1188m), where there is a *gîte*, and then by Montgros. Nasbinals has a fine Romanesque church, and from here a short 5-mile (9-km) walk leads the traveller to Aubrac, a remarkable place.

Aubrac was built in the Middle Ages by a Flemish knight who, having made the pilgrimage to Compostela, wished to help other pilgrims on the then-dangerous road across the Aubrac plateau. It's a splendid spot, still dominated by the high fortress tower, the Tour des Anglais, which now contains the *gîte d'étape,* and there is a warm welcome and good food available in the Hôtel Moderne.

The church here holds a great bell called *Maria, la cloche des perdus,* the Bell of the Lost, which was tolled each evening or during storms and fog to help the wandering pilgrim find Aubrac and shelter for the night. The tower was garrisoned by soldier monks, who harried robbers preying on the pilgrim traffic, and all in all, little Aubrac is well worth a night-stop, an evocative spot for travellers, especially in the evening as the sun goes down over the road leading out to the west, and Compostela.

After Aubrac the countryside changes and the trail starts to fall away. A long day will take the traveller off the plateau through St-Chély, and down the route of the old Roman road, which predates the pilgrim trail, to St Côme on the river Olt. The Olt is really the river Lot but it is called the Olt hereabouts, in the local *patois*. St Côme is a centre for strawberries and has plenty of good, small hotels, notably the inexpensive Voyageurs, besides marking the spot where the traveller enters the Aveyron, a modern *département* which now occupies much of what was once the Rouergue.

The trail crosses the Lot onto the southern hills and follows the river west, through some marvellously attractive old French towns, Espalion, dominated by a ruined château on the hill above, and Estaing, which has a castle right by the river, a picturesque unforgettable sight. Estaing and Espalion are towns where it pays to linger, and a day off in either place will probably prove irresistible. The passages over the river are made on bridges built by the *Frères Pontiff,* an Order which served God by building bridges for His pilgrims, a very nice, and useful, touch.

After Estaing, the footpath leaves the river and begins to climb into the remote hills of the Rouergue, and it will take two days for the walker to cross them and arrive at the end of this journey, in the town of Conques, a distance of some 24 miles (38km).

On the first day, leave Estaing following the banks of the river, to La Rouquette, and cross the bridge there to climb away to Montegut. The pattern of climbing up and down to cross a stream and then climbing up again will soon be established, but the walker who has walked this far from distant Le Puy will take this rugged country in his or her stride. The path leads on to Golinhac, a small place set high on the hill above the hot plain, where it is possible to stay in the *gîte*. The church is dedicated to St Martin and was a favourite stopping place for pilgrims both to Compostela and to the almost equally famous shrine of Ste Foy at Conques.

After Golinhac the trail heads north-west, to Espeyrac, which is a large scattered village, with accommodation available, and then climbs again to Fontromieu and then on, along the crest of the hill, until the pilgrim church of Conques comes into view on the side of the valley below. Conques is just a little place, but it has a fine hotel, the Ste Foy, a good place to celebrate the end of this journey.

Conques is a pilgrim centre in its own right and contains the shrine of Ste Foy, patron saint of prisoners. Her reliquary, and all that remains of the finest medieval treasury of Europe, can be seen in the chapter-house by the cloister. The great cathedral was protected by the abbey of Cluny, and Santiago pilgrims have flowed through here for over eight hundred years. Conques marks the end of this tour, but allow a day to see it before heading for home, or if time permits, press on along that ancient and evocative trail that comes out of history and leads to Compostela.

Walk 6 GR3 : A WALK THROUGH THE CHATEAUX COUNTRY

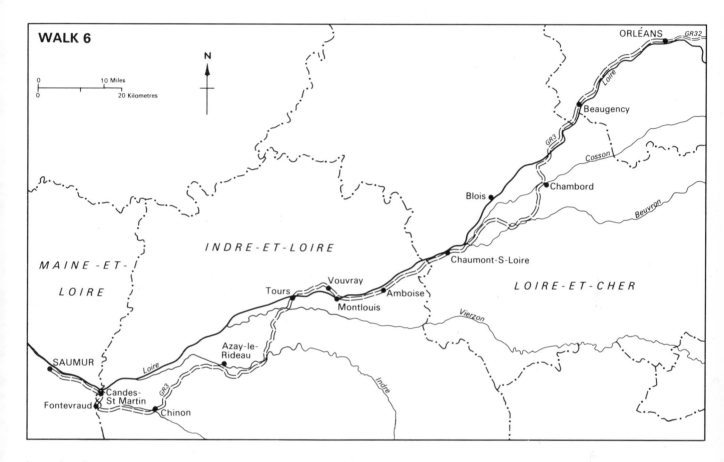

Introduction

The châteaux country of the Loire is a beautiful, classic region of France. This walk follows the river west from Orléans across the province of Touraine, the 'garden of France', into the country of Anjou, the ancestral home of the Plantagenet Kings of England. This walk is a section of the much longer GR3, *Sentier de la Loire,* which follows the river south-west on that 600-mile (1000-km) long journey from where it rises on the side of the Gerbier de Jonc in the Ardèche, to its final outpouring into the sea by St Nazaire in Brittany. This footpath crosses some beautiful and varied terrain, but no book of Classic Walks in France could choose a better section with which to illustrate the historic glories of France and French architecture.

The countryside of Touraine is what most people have in mind when they think of France. The river, blue in summer, winds between golden sandbanks; on either side stretch corn-fields or the serried soldierly ranks of the vineyards. A church steeple, black and pointed like a witch's hat, stands over the cluster of village houses, while on the hill above rise the towers of the local seigneur's château — idyllic! The Loire countryside is exactly like that, a place of dreams, somewhere to amble through, enjoying the sun, the wine, the smell of the honeysuckle. If you also enjoy art, history, architecture and romance, so much the better, for that's all they have to offer hereabouts.

In the late Middle Ages and during the High Renaissance, this land along the Loire was the hunting ground of the French Kings and their greater lords. They came here to enjoy the pleasures of the chase and avoid those plagues which ravaged Paris and kept their Court continually on the move. As a result the Loire countryside is endowed with great forests, which are still full of game, and a unique collection of great châteaux and palaces, mostly dating from

Distance: 160 miles (255km).
Time Required: Two weeks.
Type of Walk: A moderate walk through a pleasant, undemanding countryside, full of historical sites.
Maps and Guide: FFRP-CNSGR GR3 *Sentier de La Loire* (Orléans to Saumur). Michelin Green Guide: *Châteaux of the Loire.* IGN *Carte Verte* Nos. 25 & 26.
Getting to the Start: By Brittany Ferry to St Malo, then train to Orléans, or via Paris.

the sixteenth century, although they often stand on medieval foundations.

Not all these fine places are actually on the Loire. They are found as well on the tributary rivers, on the Indre and the Vienne, and not all of them are classical châteaux. Chinon on the Vienne, is medieval, a *château-fort,* the place where Joan of Arc met her *'gentil Dauphin'* in 1429, and obtained an army with which to raise the siege of Orléans. Saumur is also medieval, and appears, illustrating the month of September, in the pages of that medieval masterpiece, *Les Très Riches Heures du Duc de Berri* — but as we wander down the Loire, all this will become apparent. The trick for the visitor is to relax and enjoy it.

The best time to visit the Loire is late spring or autumn. In high summer this country is a tourist trap, with crowded hotels and long queues waiting at the gates of the châteaux. This far south it can get quite warm in summer, so

Opposite page, top: **Deer graze in the moat of the *château-fort* at Angers.**

Opposite page, bottom: **the medieval château at Saumur.**

Above: **The picturesque Chenonceaux château on a tributary of the Loire.**

Left: **Dave Wickers pauses to enjoy the sunset on the banks of the Loire.**

shorts and suncream are advisable, with something more formal to wear in the evenings, and when we were there in May, it poured with rain for a whole week! There is plenty of accommodation available, from five-star hotels to primitive camp sites, but this is not really backpackers' country; it will appeal more to those who like gentle walking, through a region of great artistic and historic interest. The path follows the river, or rivers, for much of the way and the terrain is gentle, so light equipment in a small rucksack will be perfectly adequate.

The Route

This section of the GR3 begins in the great city of Orléans, the scene of Joan of Arc's first triumph, and a very attractive town it is, well worth a day of your time. If possible, arrive around 6th May and stay for the *Fête National* on 8th May, which commemorates the burning of Joan of Arc in Rouen in 1431 and, more recently, VE-Day. There are processions and a girl dressed as *La Pucelle* herself, the Maid of Orléans, rides in armour at the head of a procession over the Loire bridges. That apart, there is much fine architecture, the Church of Notre Dame des Miracles has an ancient Black Virgin, and the riverside promenades are delightful in the evening.

The walk begins by the old bridge, on the right (north) bank of the river, and begins by following the river west, through the commercial outskirts to the village of La Chapelle-St-Mesmin, a perfect coffee stop. St Mesmin has a chapel in a grotto and a Romanesque church, and from here the path leads out, still on the north bank, towards Fourneaux. The waymarks are few, but since the route follows the towpath they are hardly needed anyway, and a further five-mile (8-km) walk will bring you to St Ay in time for lunch.

Look carefully at St Ay, for it is a place of past importance, a riverine port. Before the coming of the railways, the central Loire, now seen as a vast flood in winter, or a trickle of water through sandbanks in summer, was an industrial artery of some importance. St Ay was a port for the *chalands,* the trading sailboats of the Loire, and it still has the air and echo of those exciting times, an agreeable, peaceful little town, perfect for a leisurely lunch with friends, chatting over a little wine.

From here, the path continues along the towpath, overlooking the river all the way down to the next stop, Meung-sur-Loire, which is reached by a suspension bridge. The chief sight here is the church and castle, once the residence of the Bishops of Orléans. The poet François Villon was imprisoned and tortured here. It is also a wine centre and the local wine, although quite unknown outside the district, is very drinkable.

After Meung, the river and the towpath make a brief swing to the south, across the vineyards, following a bend in the river, returning to meet yet another attractive little town at Beaugency, another medieval town, captured by the English in 1428 and recaptured by St Joan in the following year. The Huguenots burned it in 1567 but much still remains to please the eye, notably the fine castle of Joan's great captain and colleague, Dunois, the Bastard of Orléans, which now contains the regional museum. All in all, Beaugency is a place to explore and linger in, perhaps overnight, before pressing on west, into a less populated countryside, through Lestiou to Muides-sur-Loire, where the path leaves the north bank, crosses the river and turns along the south bank to St Dye, a nice little town, once a stop for pilgrims coming from Paris on that Pilgrim Road to Compostela.

At St Dye the GR3 leaves the Loire, at least for a while, and plunges south, across one of those greating hunting forests, heading for the first of our great Renaissance châteaux, Chambord. Finding the way through these forests is not always easy. The path runs through wide rides and they are obvious, but what is less obvious is which ride to take at the various junctions or roundabouts *(carrefour);* close attention to the instruction in the *Topo-Guide* can save miles on this section. The path leads at last to the *Sentier du parc de Chambord,* and across the little river Cosson to the château itself.

It took many years, and the wealth of two Kings, François I and Henri II, to complete the building of Chambord, which is one of the marvels of the French Renaissance. The wall of the park is twenty miles round, and the palace itself is vast, and yet this, you should realise, is a hunting lodge; some hunting lodge! Louis XIV gave masques and balls here, and the modern *Son-et-Lumière* performances are worth seeing.

Visiting Chambord will require at least half a day, so stay the night locally before setting out next day across the forest of Boulogne to Clenard, a small attractive village, typical of the Sologne. From here the path runs west, skirting the Forêt de Russy to Cellettes, a little town where the path turns north into the forest again, along rides to the track junction at the *Carrefour de l'Etoile.* One interesting diversion off this route is to the castle of Beauregard, overlooking the banks of the Beuvron to the south, a fine little place and another, much smaller, hunting lodge built by François I.

At the *Carrefour de l'Etoile,* deep in the

forest, the walker has a choice, to head for the château of Chaumont, or divert to the city of Blois. Personally I would recommend the *variante,* for Blois is a very fine provincial city, and one that should not be missed. Besides, the actual diversion is only 4 miles (6km) and the path can easily be rejoined on foot or by taking a bus back to it after visiting the city. The château at Blois is very interesting and noted as the place where Henri III had the Duc de Guise assassinated in 1588. After visiting Blois, take the bus and rejoin the GR3 at Chailles, 5 miles (8km) further down river.

Those who remain with the GR3 will leave the forest at Chailles and turn west for Cande-sur-Beuvron, skirting the Loire, before arriving at another grand château, the palace of Chaumont. This belonged to Henri II's Queen, Catherine de Medici, but after his death in a tournament, she exchanged it for the even more splendid château at Chenonceaux, which Henri had given to his mistress, the beguiling Diane de Poitiers. Chaumont stands in a parkland, a fair walk in from the gate, and those who just want to look at it can do so more easily from the bridge which leads across the Loire to Onzain.

Otherwise, after visiting the château, follow the path along the south bank of the river, and down to the town of Amboise, 12 miles (21km) further west. Like Blois, Amboise will repay a visit. Leonardo da Vinci lived here; Charles VIII died here; hundreds of Huguenots were murdered here — it's that sort of place, reeking of history.

The path goes on to the west, a little inland from the Loire now, to Lussault and Montlouis, where it re-crosses the Loire onto the north bank and into the town of Vouvray, which is famous for a fine white wine, and is a good stopping place before the next major town on this journey, the city of Tours, the capital of the province of Touraine.

The path enters Tours from Rochecorbon where the abbey of Marmoutier was founded in the fourth century by one of France's favourite saints, St Martin of Tours. Todays Tours is the major city of Central France, very busy, very commercial, full of hotels and restaurants, but with plenty of camp sites in the outskirts. Do not leave without exploring the town, visiting the basilica of St Martin and, on the western outskirts, the fine château of Plessis-lès-Tours.

Tours occupies much of the land between the Loire and a tributary river, the Cher, and the GR3 footpath begins again at the St Sauveur bridge over the Cher, in the south of the city. Cross this bridge and turn west, following the river for a little way before entering the woods west of Joué-lès-Tours (*lès* means 'near') and

turning south for Ballan-Mire, 5 miles (8km) away.

Legend has it that Ballan, and not Poitiers was the place where Charles Martel, of course with the aid of St Martin, defeated the Saracens in 778 AD and so saved Europe for the Christians. The path skirts Ballan, and presses on across the pleasant country of Touraine, a mixture of fields and woodland, to Artannes on the river Indre, then to Pont-de-Ruan, Saché, and along the crest of a shallow valley to La Vallée, before turning north again for the Indre and La Chapelle-St-Blaise. It is possible to cut out this wide swing by leaving the footpath at Le Gué-Droit and carrying on west along the Indre, for La Chapelle-St-Blaise and the château of Azay-le-Rideau.

Azay is a small classic, moated château which lies only one kilometre off the GR3 and should certainly not be missed.

At Cheille, a few miles to the west, one of the early Counts of Anjou built a monastery, of which little remains except the later thirteenth-century church, but it's a quiet, pleasant spot. From there a good day's walk across the forests follows the GR3 south and west, from the Indre to the river Vienne and into the fortress town of Chinon.

Chinon is a splendid place, especially to those many people who like to feel the echoes of a medieval world. The Plantagenet Counts of Anjou built the first castle here, on the heights above the north bank, and for the most impressive view of the castle, cross the river bridge

Top: **A trail through the hunting forest on the way to Chambord. Although wide and obvious, these trails are numerous and so careful map reading is necessary to avoid getting lost.**

Above: **Sunset on the Loire.**

Chinon is full of medieval buildings, little alleys, cobbled streets and quiet squares. There are a number of hotels along the river promenade, and a good camp site by the bridge on the far side of the river.

A night in Chinon is an excellent idea, and from there a long but quite possible walk of some 22 miles (33km) will bring the walker to the end of the journey at Saumur inside a day. On the way we come to Fontevraud and it might be as well to stay a night there, but ring ahead and book for accommodation at Fontevraud is not plentiful and often crowded.

Leave Chinon by crossing the bridge to the south bank and turning west along the Vienne, casting a last look back at the castle. The first miles, to La Chaussée, are flat and rather dull, but there the footpath turns south and passes through woods to the village of Fontevraud, another essential stop on this historic journey. In the early Middle Ages, the Plantagenet Counts of Anjou, who later became Kings of England, built the monastery here at Fontevraud. It became their favourite religious foundation, and the mausoleum of the dynasty. In the great church you can see the partly-gilded effigies of such famous figures as Eleanor of Aquitaine, Henry II of England, her husband, their mighty son, Richard Coeur-de-Lion, and Isabelle of Angoulême, the much neglected wife of King John, he whom the French still call Jean Sans-Terre, John Lackland. There are guided tours around the abbey, and waiting for one to start takes time, but like so many places on this walk, the abbey at Fontevraud cannot really be missed by any lover of history and fine architecture.

From here the GR path turns north again and rejoins the Vienne just before Candes-St-Martin, where it flows into the Loire. From here the path veers up to and away from the river, through Dampierre, until the castle of Saumur comes into sight.

Saumur is a fine town, devoted to the horse. The French Cavalry have their Armoured School there, and the horse squadron, the *Cadre Noir,* still presents spectacular displays throughout the summer. The castle contains a fine Museum of the Horse, and there, beside the high white walls, we end this walk through the green country of the Loire and the historic heartland of France.

without looking back, then turn quickly for that first stunning sight of the castle. Closer inspection will reveal that all that remains of Chinon is but a shell, but this is the place to which the captain of Vaucouleurs brought Joan of Arc, and from where she began the campaigns which eventually, by 1454, drove the English out of France and finally put an end to the Hundred Years War. If the castle above is a disappointment, the town below is a delight.

Walk 7 THE ROAD OF THE TEMPLARS AND KNIGHTS HOSPITALLERS

Introduction

This walk, the GR71C, *Chemin des Templiers et Hospitaliers,* is a short but delightful 50-mile (80-km) walk across some of the most beautiful country in France — delightful that is, if you like the high, wild, open places. It leads the walker at a gentle pace to some fascinating relics of the Middle Ages, beginning and ending at the walled town of La Couvertoirade, which was built by the Knights Templar in the middle of the twelfth century, seized by the officers of King Philip le Bel after the Templars were suppressed early in the fourteenth century, and handed at the orders of Pope Clement to the Knights of St John of Jerusalem, otherwise known as the Hospitallers. That medieval gem

apart, the walk visits other once famous places, like Ste. Eulalie with its splendid church, Viala-de-Pas-de-Jaux, which was another *Commanderie* or headquarters for the Templars, and the old *mas* or farmhouse at Baldy.

Such places apart though, the chief attraction of this walk is the countryside through which it passes. The land is high, on or over the 3280-ft (1000m) mark for much of the way, and although the route descends into valleys, much of the way lies over the high windy tableland of the *causse.* This is sheep country, short-grassed, open, treeless. Water is scanty, and in high summer there is little shelter from the sun. I think it's delightful, for this is the sort of country

The open landscape of the Causse du Larzac.

65

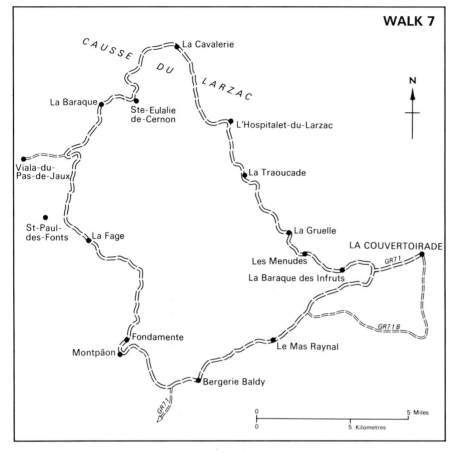

The Route

The Chemin begins at La Couvertoirade, but the walk should not start without a tour of this little medieval *bourg,* which has changed very little in the last seven hundred years. Most of the streets are still unpaved, the fortifications are largely intact, and the old houses, now restored, have been taken over as workshops by craftsmen and artists. Outside the walls, notice the *lavogne* or dewpond, which is still used to water the flocks of sheep which graze on the *causse.* Water is scarce up here, and needed for the sheep, whose milk goes to make the cheese which matures in the nearby caves at Roquefort. During the Middle Ages, the Templars and the Hospitallers used this fortress as a base from which they hunted down robbers and the mercenary Free-Companies which ravaged France during the Hundred Years War.

From the *bourg* go west, along the minor road for a short way, until the road swings left and the footpath begins, running west across the *causse,* through some small hills. The GR71C often uses a direct route across the *causse,* with no apparent footpath to follow, so it is essential to either use a map and compass, or pay particular attention to the red and white waymarks. These tend to fade quickly in the sun, but were fresh and vivid in the summer of 1983.

The path joins up briefly with a minor road, the D185, to turn north for a short distance, before heading north-west across the *causse* to the little roadside hamlet of La Baraque des Infruts.

The path goes straight through Baraque, across the main road and out again, on the dirt track to a small farm, then west on a footpath to Les Menudes, a little cluster of golden stone farm buildings then onto a track before veering off across open country to La Gruelle. The path is, or was, invisible, but the waymarks, red and white splashes on the stones, are frequent and as the La Gruelle farm is the only place on the *causse* to the north, it cannot really be missed. The *causse* here is really just a grassy desert, a void of space and sky.

La Gruelle lies at the end of a track which leads east to the main N9 road, which the footpath parallels for some miles, heading north and a little east for L'Hospitalet. Note the *lavogne* at La Gruelle, as you leave, and quit the footpath after a short distance to strike directly north, using the high ground ahead as an aiming point for your compass. After about a kilometre the walker should cross a minor road, the D65, and then, past the remains of a prehistoric shelter at La Traoucade, from which a track leads up to the village of L'Hospitalet-du-Larzac.

Distance: 50 miles (80 km)
Time: One week.
Type of Walk: A gentle walk across rolling open country, over the Causse de Larzac.
Season: Late spring — September to October.
Maps and Guides: FFRP-CNSGR GR71C *Chemin des Templiers et Hospitaliers.* Map IGN *Carte Verte* No. 64.
Getting to the Start: By train and bus via Millau.

you cannot find in Britain.

The GR71C *Topo-Guide* divides the route into eleven stages of between 4 and 5 miles (7 and 9km), which are rather too short, even for a loaded, well-equipped backpacker. In fact, the walk can easily be completed in five days or less, although the sights along the way deserve consideration, and some moments of your time.

The weather in spring and autumn will be mild or pleasantly warm, but nights are often cold at this height, and a set of warm clothing and windproofs would be advisable. Light boots or trainers should be worn and since the paths are often faint, a compass will be useful, as will an extra water bottle, and some freeze-dried rations.

Accommodation is not plentiful, and it is best to camp, although if camping wild, permission should be obtained if possible from the shepherds or local farmers. There is a large well-equipped camp site just south of l'Hospitalet, a *gîte d'étape* at La Couvertoirade, and hotels at La Cavalerie and Montpaon.

This walk is actually a *variante* of the much longer GR71, Cévennes-Languedoc, and the perfect introduction to a part of France which most visitors never get to see.

The camp site here lies a little to the south of the village, just off the N9. L'Hospitalet is fairly large as places go on the *causse,* and was founded by Guilbert of Millau, the local Seigneur, in 1108.

Leave L'Hospitalet past the church by the D23 road which runs through some woods to the western escarpment, and turn off at a road junction, to head north on a dirt track through the wood. The local aerodrome will be in sight to the right from time to time, and the land falls away sharply to the left. This track passes another *lavogne,* and goes onto the N9 before entering La Cavalerie.

La Cavalerie is bigger than L'Hospitalet, and owes much of its present prosperity to the nearby Army camp. There are several hotels and restaurants, some remnants of the medieval fortifications, and one or two pleasant bars, if they are not overcrowded by the rough soldiery.

To leave La Cavalerie, follow the N9 north for a few hundred metres, turning off to the left *before* the wayside cross, on a track which leads south-west, and starts to descend at first gently, and then quite steeply, into the valley of the river Cernon, a wide valley, very different, and warmer, than the plateau of the *causse* above. The track leads to the farm at Le Frayssinet, and then down into the western outskirts of the village of Ste-Eulalie-de-Cernon. Take the road north-west here, towards Lapanouse, turning off just past the pumping station, to climb up the south side of the valley towards La Baraque, with the peak of Cougouille, 2990ft (912m), the highest point on the Causse de Larzac, off to the left.

From La Baraque follow the path and the waymarks to La Carbonnière, on the crest of the southern ridge. South and west of here, the path joins up with a minor road, and a short distance to the west, past a small cemetery lies the village of Viala-du-Pas-de-Jaux, another stronghold of the Templars.

After Viala, which is certainly worth a look, the path heads briefly east then leaves all roads behind and plunges south, skirting the cliffs to the west which encircle the village of St-Paul-des Fonts, and arrives at the farm of La Fage, which has yet another *lavogne.* From here the path continues to skirt the cliffs, passes through Louradouberg and then descends through the woods to the hamlets of Fondamente and, on the hill behind, Montpaon, with its ruined castle. These two villages can provide plenty of accommodation and a chance to restock with food and water.

The next stage of this journey over the *causse* is across some steep wooded country, where zigzag paths mix with those across small hilltop

plateaux. The path climbs steadily from Montpaon to the Pas Farrat, and crosses the high *and waterless* Guilhaumand plateau, south of the Rocher de l'Aigle, which walkers should beware of in bad weather, to the farm or *mas* at Bergerie Baldy. From here the route is fairly even and easy to follow, skirting the rim of the escarpment with fine views out to the north, and following this crest most of the way east to Le

Top: **The unique natural wonder of the Cirque de Navacelles on the causse.**

Above: **The Templar town of La Couvertoirade.**

67

A dew pond or *lavogne* – the main source of water on the causse not only for sheep but for walkers too.

A stone cross marks the way on the *Chemin des Templars*.

Mas Raynal.

Le Mas Raynal is really more of a hamlet than an isolated farm, and from this point on the GR path becomes clear again as the country opens out and assumes the more familiar features of the high *causse*. At Canals, another footpath *variante,* the GR71B turns off by the cemetery and heads south, but we are now on the GR71 proper, and it follows or shares the route of the minor D140 north and east to La Pézade on the N9.

La Pézade is just a little south of La Baraque des Infructs, which was our first aiming point on this walk, and from here the path heads east across low hills, climbing to just over 2625ft (800m), until the towers of La Couvertoirade come again into sight and this tour of the empty Causse de Larzac is over.

Walk 8 DRAILLE ROADS OF THE CEVENNES

Above and below: **A *draille* road and walkers in the Cévennes**

Introduction

Can one really have too much of a good thing? Proverbs and sayings put aside, I doubt it, for today good things are usually hard to find. Besides, as far as walkers are concerned, if an area is attractive to them, there is usually a good reason for it. Walkers flock to the Peaks and the Lakes, not to find other walkers but because the walking there is superb — and so it is with the Cévennes.

Those who wander into the Cévennes, perhaps at the end of the Robert Louis Stevenson Trail, will find these hills enchanting and, more relevant to this book, very different from anything available here in Britain. Our chosen route follows many ancient and therefore classic routes, the *drailles,* or drove-

roads of Southern France, still used to drive sheep and cattle along to market. The Cévennes are rugged, stony, hot, often flayed by forest fires, covered with the scrub oaks of the *garrigue,* scented with gorse and honeysuckle, vivid, not easy to walk in but certainly unforgettable and a place to return to again and again.

When I first visited the Cévennes I was struck by the fact that the river Gardon seemed to flow everywhere. Eventually the man in the tourist office at Alès put my mind at rest by explaining that there were, in fact, *seven* Gardons, all tributaries of the greater river Gard. Curious, and confusing, but useful to know.

This walk of 80 miles (130km) circles the valleys of these various Gardons, and takes in

Distance: 80 miles (130km).
Time required: One week.
Type of walk: A hill-walk over rugged country, suitable for fit walkers or backpackers.
Maps and Guides: FFRP-GR67 *Sentier du Tour des Cévennes*. Michelin Green Guide: *Gorges du Tarn*. IGN Carte 1:100,000 *Parc National des Cévennes*.
Getting to the Start: Via Nîmes or Montpellier to Alès, Anduze (Gard) or via Mende (Lozère).

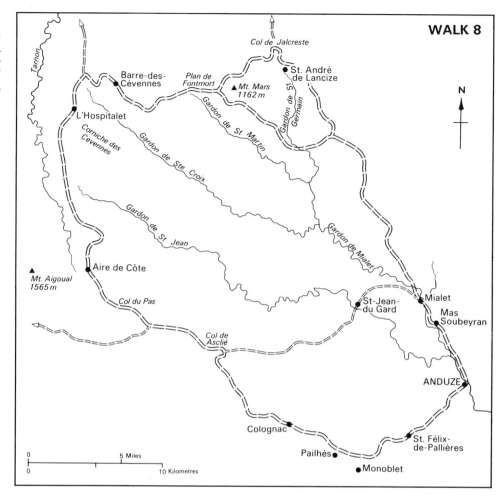

most, if not all, of the finest parts of the Cévennes, and notably those places where walkers will gather. It runs through Barre-des-Cévennes, by the Col de Jalcreste, into Anduze and along the eastern slopes of Mont Aigoual — all combining to create the perfect walk for the fit hill-walker.

It cannot be an easy walk and the difficulties will vary with the time of year. There can be snow about in the spring, and the nights are chilly outside in high summer, when the days will become very hot indeed. The ground underfoot is rough and stony, so that good boots or *very* thick-soled trainers are advisable. Accommodation is fairly plentiful, even in summer, with small hotels, *gîtes d'étape* and camp sites in plenty, so this walk should appeal to all kinds of walker, but perhaps especially to the backpacker. We suggest that you should take a tent and be self-sufficient.

The Route

The trail begins in the little town of Anduze,

in the south of the country. Leaving Anduze the trail starts with a sweep to the south-west, on the route followed by an even longer Randonnée path, the GR6 (Alpes-Océan), winding along the valley and rising fairly slowly through the scrub oaks and pine trees to the village of St Felix-de-Pallières, 4 miles (6.5km) away, which has a *gîte d'étape*. From here, continue west, through open, hilly country, ignoring the little *variante* to Monoblet, skirting the round hill of La Barthe to the north and into Pailhès. The route from here runs close to the D185 minor road to the Col du Rédarès 1250ft (381m), which marks the boundary into the Park National des Cévennes.

Follow the track west and descend to the village of Colognac, 4 miles (6km) away which has a *gîte d'étape* and a camp site, and would therefore be a good place to stop for the first night and get sorted out.

Colognac lies at 1970ft (600m) and marks the point at which the path starts to climb as it turns north towards the open slopes of Mont Aigoual, 5135ft (1565m). The rise is gradual, for the path follows the contours wherever possible, but the ascent is nevertheless perceptible. The path follows the valley of the Livan through Le Fabre, and over the col which carries one of the great drove roads of the Languedoc, the *Draille de la Margeride*, past the deserted village at Les Fosses and so to the crest of the ridge at a point called Camp Barrat, a breezy spot with fine views, at 3000ft (915m).

From here the path pushes up to the north to the long ridge of the Montagne du Liron at 3285ft (1001m) and picks up the *draille* along the ridge which contours at the 3280-ft (1000-m) mark east and north to yet another col, the Col du Fageas, another open spot with marvellous views. The tip of the Liron at 3865ft (1178m), lies just a little to the east, and it can be scaled with ease.

From here the *draille* descends abruptly to the road at the Col de l'Asclie, from where there is a short walk to the Col de l'Homme Mort. From L'Asclie, another footpath, the GR61, heads north-east to the end of Stevenson's journey, at St-Jean-du-Gard. Our route, though, lies to the west, although there is another long *variante* south to Notre Dame de la Rouvière, and then back to the GR67 at Bonperrier, our next destination.

From the Col de l'Asclie, the *draille* runs along the ridge to another col, the ominously-named Col de l'Homme Mort, and then follows the north slope of the col to Bonperrier. Just north of this route lies the farmhouse known as the Mas Soubeyran, a centre for the Camisards during their wars against the King's Army during the eighteenth century.

From Bonperrier the *draille* follows the crest, at round the 2950ft (900m) mark to the Col du Pas, where a minor road, the D10, crosses over the mountain, and then climbs again to Le Pas at 3540ft (1080m), where a wide forest track comes in from the east and leads down to the hamlet at Aire de Côte. This point is overlooked by the heights of Mont Aigoual to the west, and a diversion to climb this mountain may well prove irresistible. The Aire forms a watershed where some streams flow north, to the Atlantic, and others south into the Gard, and so to the Mediterranean. It also meets the point where the GR6 departs to the west, and our route picks up that of another very long footpath, the GR7 (Vosges-Pyreneés) which it follows, still on the *draille* to the Col Salides 3415ft (1014m). The route from the Aire de Côte offers a choice of paths on either side of the Serre du Tarnon, amounting almost to another *variante,* but all paths lead to the Col Salides, where yet another minor road, the D19, crosses over the mountain.

From Col Salides the path runs north through countryside that is pure Cévennes, opening out

Cirque de St Chély

to encapsulate all that is best of this always beautiful region, up to the hamlet at L'Hospitalet at the head of the road that runs down to St-Jean-du-Gard, across the high *Corniche des Cévennes*. This was the first place I visited in the Cévennes, and I can still remember it, open, cloud-capped, beautiful and so far, marvellously unspoilt.

The *draille* follows the crest north out of the rugged country we have followed for the last few days onto a windy upland plateau, almost a small *causse*. As usual, the path crosses another col, the Col du Marquaires, and on under the lee of the small hill to the east at Point 1111 into L'Hospitalet. The views on the way are spectacular, to the Causse Méjean, into the Tarnon valley and down on scattered hamlets and small, deserted farms.

L'Hospitalet is a little place founded, as the

This rugged hill-side on the GR67 almost obscures the path which can be seen half way up the slope.

name implies, by the Knights Hospitallers. There is a *gîte d'étape* and camping is possible, so a day off here would be enjoyable before setting off for the next long leg, through part of the way by road to Barre-des-Cévennes, which is practically a town with several hotels and a restaurant, a good place for lunch at the end of a vigorous morning.

At Barre-des-Cévennes the walker has turned the corner of the most northern part of the path and from now on the trail runs east or south to Anduze, with an interesting walk to start this second leg, to Plan de Fontmort, part of which follows a hill road, the D13. From here the path veers off the D13 to the left and heads east towards the slopes of the Mont Mars at 3810ft (1162m), where a *variante* heads south to the Col de la Pierre Plantée. We follow the true path to the north, to the Col des Laupies 3285ft (1001m), and then to another of those high points for walkers in France, the Col de Jalcreste. This actually lies a few hundred metres north of the waymarked route, but footpaths run off in all directions at this point and it makes a good lunch stop. Here too, the GR67 picks up another *draille*, the *Draille de*

Gevaudan, which contours south around St André de Lancize to the scattered hamlet at Les Ayres and south to Le Pradel. This route follows a very ancient drove road known as the *Grande Draille du Languedoc,* which stays at the 2950-ft (900-m) mark. There is, therefore, no shelter other than wild camping when night comes on. Past Le Pradel the path descends slightly to around 2625ft (800m), and along the crest to the farm at Le Pereyret. From now on the path, though never exactly level, contours to descend steadily. The next col is only at 1930ft (528m), and the *draille* continues south on forest tracks, crossing various small streams into the valley of a Gardon at Aigladines.

This particular river is known as the Gardon de Mialet and the path descends to the south to the bridge at Pont des Camisards and so into the town of Mialet. This valley is full of little hotels, *gîtes,* camp sites and contains, at Mas Soubeyran, the *Musée du Désert,* which tells the story of the Camisard revolt.

From here the end of the path lies only a few kilometres away, back again in the pretty town of Anduze.

Walk 9 A TOUR OF THE VOLCANO COUNTRY

Introduction

Of all the varying scenery which France can offer the walker, the Chaîne des Puys, the northern part of the country's Massif Central core of highlands, must rank among the most distinctive. There is no landscape in Britain that comes even near to it. The secret behind the unusual shape of the terrain is rooted not in climate but in geology. The 'chain' is a string of volcanoes, long since extinct but still of unmistakable origin even to those who saw their last volcano in the pages of a school geography textbook. The French call the area a 'museum of volcanic forms'.

The shapes are classic. The range, which stretches in an almost dead straight line from the village of Le Viallard in the north to Saulzet le Froid in the south (just a few kilometres to the west of Clermont-Ferrand) is formed from the plugs of volcanoes which erupted some twenty-five million years (or more) ago, and offers an abrupt, unexpected mass of contour in an otherwise moderately flat-plain landscape. For the benefit of those who are able to visualize landscapes from statistics, the twenty major and nearly eighty minor humps amount to some eight cubic kilometres of lava matter. Several are capped by craters which, even though carpeted with a gentle blanket of greenery, are bound to conjure up fantasies of bubbling infernos; except, of course, those which are

Part of the distinctive line of volcanoes that make up the Chaîne des Puys.

73

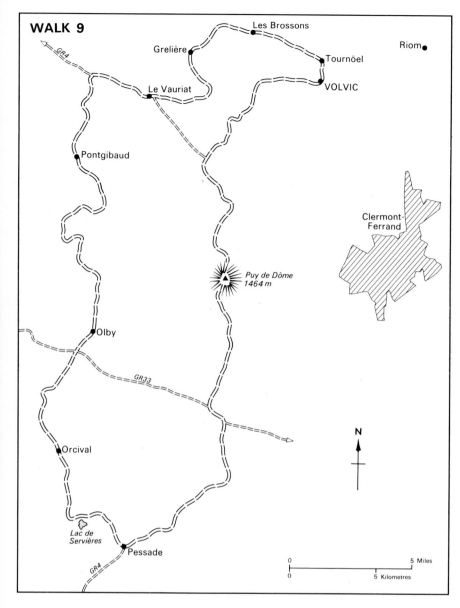

WALK 9

Les Brossons

Grelière

Riom

Tournöel

Le Vauriat

VOLVIC

GR4

Pontgibaud

Clermont-Ferrand

Puy de Dôme
1464 m

Olby

GR33

N

Orcival

Lac de
Servières

Pessade

GR4

0						5 Miles

0   5 Kilometres

Distance: 65 miles (108km).
Time required: Five to seven days.
Type of walk: Not a difficult trek, although there are plenty of ups and downs.
Season: Early spring and late autumn.
Maps and Guides: FFPR-CNSGR GR441 *Tour de la Chaîne des Puys. Portrait of the Auvergne* by Peter Graham (Hale). IGN *Carte Verte* 1:100,000 No. 49.
Getting to the Start: By train to Clermont-Ferrand (or air) and then to Volvic Railway Station.

filled with water — there are fifteen lakes in and around the *chaîne*, some in craters, others formed by the cooling lava flows that blocked the ends of the valleys. One of the best examples is the Lake of Servières, just to the south of Vernines, which occupies a volcanic crater surrounded by a forest of pines.

The Route

The GR441 is a circular route and the *Topo-Guide,* as usual, follows it in either direction. The eastern leg is the one closest to the route's original *raison d'être*. It twists and turns, but basically adheres to the north-south line of the *chaîne,* climbing to the tops of five volcanoes (including the 4800ft (1464m) Puy de Dôme)

and weaving a slalom course between the rest. Because the slopes of the hills are mostly tree-covered, with pines and silver birch, it is only from the summits that you can enjoy the full perspective of this unusual landscape.

The western section, which is roughly twice as long as the *chaîne* route, passes through villages with plenty of good grazing and forested countryside, well endowed with rivers, although basically it is a vast, empty region with a scant population. If you have the time and enjoy walking circular routes, cover it all, but if you are merely keen on seeing the main sights, then keep to the linear La Viallard to Saulzet-le-Froid section, or an even shorter compromise between Puy de la Nugère and Montlosier. If time is limited you will find a few short cuts to make a smaller circuit, namely the GR4 from Le Vauriat to Puy Chopine and the GR33 near Les Plates. For further information on the shorter route obtain the locally sold *'25 Circuits dans les Dômes'*, edited by Chamina.

Wind and waterproof clothing is essential for the *chaîne,* even in summer. The *Topo-Guide* aptly describes the Auvergne climate as 'rude', and short, sharp showers are to be expected, simply because the hills constitute the first significant barrier to the predominantly water-laden westerlies. Warm clothing should also be carried, plus a windproof shell for the more exposed sections. Fog can harass your journey, especially in the eastern Puys section, so a compass is necessary. Carry water in this section too, as there are several long, dry gaps. The *Topo-Guide* also recommends that you take along an anti-snake-bite preparation as a precautionary measure against snake bite during the summer when the reptiles enjoy basking on the exposed slopes of the Puys.

The GR441 can begin at any point, for it is a circular tour, but Volvic in the north-east corner, near Riom, is a good starting point, and the one listed in the *Topo-Guide*. From here the trail heads west to Les Brossons, past the castle at Tournoël, and then weaves among the volcanic hills to Grelière and Le Vauriat, where it links with the GR4. West of here the trail turns due south and runs for two or three days, all the way to the Lac de Servières, before turning east through Pessade and heading north, to the east of Clermont-Ferrand, through or over a thick cluster of high-coned volcanic hills, over the very top of the Puy de Dôme, 4800ft (1464m), and a final, long and windy run to the end of the tour at Volvic.

Apart from the rare beauty of the scenery, the GR441 will lead you to several interesting man-made places, although it must be emphasised that the villages on this tour can hardly be

described as pretty. The dark stone and fairly sombre clusters of buildings, as well as the isolated stone farmhouses with their distinctive stone-tiled roofs, are a matter of acquired taste rather than instant delight. Most are constructed from the dark volcanic lava rock called *andesite,* an easily-worked but durable material which has been widely used in the area since the Middle Ages and is still mined at, for example, Volvic.

Soon after you leave Volvic, heading north, you come to the remains of a rather grand feudal castle at Tournoël, one of the most important in the Auvergne. Its history dates back to the tenth century, and it belonged to the Counts of the Auvergne, although what we see today are the romantic hilltop ruins of fourteenth-century reconstruction and fortification and the more recent embellishments such as the gothic doorways, fancy windows and Italianate gardens, a seventeenth-century attempt to transform it into an impressive, if less bellicose, home.

The area around Pontgibaud was well known to the Romans, who established a village by the town above the flood plain of the river Sioule, near to the site of the present-day railway station. Their main interest, and that of subse-

quent residents, was the mining of silver, an industry which ground to a halt at the end of the last century as the minerals became exhausted. Orcival, a small village in the wooded valley of

Top: **The Parc des Volcans in the Auvergne.**

Above: **Mont Dore from which more of the twenty major and nearly eighty minor volcanic humps can be seen.**

the Sioulet at the foot of Le Mont Dore, contains a beautiful, twelfth-century Romanesque church. It has an octagonal bell tower with several round chapels spilling around the base, while its most revered interior feature is the twelfth-century Virgin in Majesty behind the altar.

South of Olby, just to the east of the hamlet of St Martin de Tours, you will come across the château of Cordes, dating back to the thirteenth century and restored in the seventeenth. Apart from being famous it is worth visiting for its gardens of box and yew hedges, landscaped by Le Nôtre.

One of the oldest sites along the trail is sited in the most dramatic of all locations; the ruins of the Roman temple of Mercury are to be found on the summit of the Puy de Dôme itself, in the shadow of a more modern observatory, TV transmitter and restaurant. The spectacular position, its solitude and difficult access, all explain why the Puy de Dôme has long been looked upon with spiritual reverence, and its religious history includes sorcerers and black magic rituals dating back to the worship of the god Lug, as well as more conventional religious practices. Today the crowds who make the pilgrimage to the summit come simply to admire the view — on a clear day you can see not only a hundred volcanic summits, but also eleven *départements* of France. Apart from such occasional sights, it is the countryside through which the GR441 travels which really puts man into insignificant perspective. This is a route for anyone who relishes the thought of a few, not unstrenuous, days in geographically alien surroundings, so alien, that despite the extra weight, it would be fun to carry and consult a basic layman's guidebook to the whys and wherefores of volcanoes.

If that sounds too scientific for a walker, then settle for the speculative comments made by Alexandre Vialatte on the origins of this unique region: 'When God had created the World, on the eighth day he created the Auvergne and the Auvergnat, offering him all the treasures of the earth . . . And the Lord pointed out that the volcanoes were still active. 'No matter' said the Auvergnat, 'they will cool, and I can wait.' As you will see, they are worth waiting for.

Top: **The volcanic craters are ideal take-off points for hang gliders.**

Middle: **The 1464-metre Puy-de-Dôme.**

Bottom: **Looking across to Clermont-Ferrand through the valley mist.**

Walk 10 THE TRO-BREIZ : TOUR OF BRITTANY TRAIL

Introduction

The Tro-Breiz, Tour of Brittany footpath, the GR34, is a very long path, reaching into all parts of the province and covered by no less than four *Topo-Guides*. The total route at present, with the numerous *variantes,* already covers some hundreds of miles and it is still expanding, but the section here, from Huelgoat in the Argoat, the 'country of wood', to the fishing port of Douarnenez in Armorica, the 'land facing the sea', takes in two contrasting parts of the province, and in wandering west towards the Atlantic, it manages to include some splendid parts of Brittany, both man-made and natural. Brittany has always been very popular with the British and no book of Classic Walks could omit this famous province.

This short section of the longer path crosses Finistère to the west, and then turns south along the cliff paths of the coast and across the wide estuary of the Aulne, a great salmon fishing river. This part of Brittany can often be wet and windy due to the moisture imparted by the Atlantic winds, but it is therefore also very green and pleasant, with marvellous views along the rocky coast and out to offshore islands from the tops of the various hills which lie along the route.

The walk can be made at any time outside the deep winter months, and should appeal to all kinds of walker, from the casual stroller to the well-equipped backpacker. Light boots are quite adequate, but rainproof clothing is highly advisable.

A typical Breton port.

77

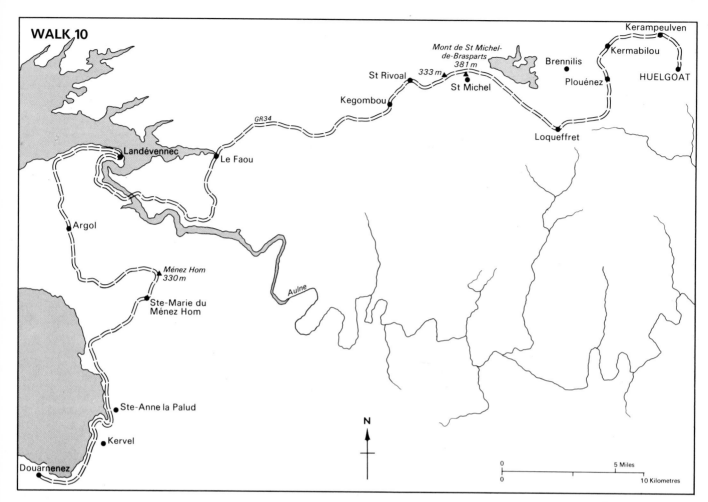

WALK 10

GR34

Kerampeulven
Kermabilou
HUELGOAT
Brennilis
Plouénez
Mont de St Michel-
de-Brasparts
381 m
St Michel
St Rivoal
333 m
Loqueffret
Kegombou
Le Faou
Landévennec
Argol
Ménez Hom
330 m
Aulne
Ste-Marie du
Ménez Hom
Ste-Anne la Palud
Kervel
Douarnenez

N

0 ⌞_____⌟ 5 Miles
0 ⌞_____⌟ 10 Kilometres

Distance: 80 miles (130 km)
Time Required: One week.
Type of Walk: A gentle cross-country walk over moderate terrain for lightly equipped walkers.
Maps and Guides: FFPR-CNSGR GR34 *Tro-Breiz.* IGN *Carte Verte* Nos. 13, 14, 15. *Michelin Green Guide to Brittany. A Visitor's Guide to Brittany,* (Moorland Publishing).
Getting to the Start: By Brittany Ferry to St Malo or Roscoff, then by train to Huelgoat.

Across the causeway to Mont-St-Michel.

The Route

Huelgoat is *the* walker's centre in Brittany, popular with day walkers and well provided with trails, a little town snug in the woods, set around a lake and backed by a chaotic mass of tumbled rocks. It would be a good idea to begin this walk with a day's walking in the woods around Huelgoat, and so get ready for the main GR 34. There are plenty of small hotels and a nice camp site here, and a restful day will put you in the right mood for a restful, relaxing walk.

The walk begins with a stretch to the north over the low crest of the hills and up to the menhir, or standing stone, at Kerampeulven, on a mixture of forest paths and country lanes, as is much of the route. The path gradually swings to the west, into more open country, then swings south past Kermabilou (*ker* in Breton means place), and eventually down to Plouénez, past another menhir, and the hamlet of Brennilis, which is worth a diversion, if only to see the dolmen called the 'House of the Dwarfs', and for fine views across the lake towards the hill of St-Michel-de-Brasparts.

The path here is gentle and fairly easy to follow, apart from some narrow places in the scrubland, past Keranou, down to St Herbot and the remains of the railway station at Loqueffret, at the foot of a low local hill called the Ménez-Du. This can be climbed but it is only a few more miles to one of the high spots of Brittany, the Mont de Saint-Michel-de-Brasparts. There are no real mountains in Brittany, and at 1250ft (381m), or just under 1000ft (304m), this is the best we can do, but the views from the top are superb. On the way to the summit, which is crowned by St Michel's Chapel, walkers will find a group of stones called the *Eured Veign*, or Stone Wedding, which according to local legend are the remains of a wedding party who were turned into stone for annoying the local priest.

Once off St Michel, down past the 1090-ft (333-m) spot-mark, the path picks up and then follows a minor road to the little village of St

Pointe de Raz on the Brittany coast marks the end of the walk.

d'Armorique. The country is hilly, a mixture of wood and heathland, and the path can be muddy, so gaiters should be worn. Since accommodation is scanty on this section of the road, wise walkers will do it in a day and reward themselves with a day off in Le Faou, a very pretty spot. Le Faou is not very big but when the tide is in and the sun goes down across the sea to the west, casting pink rays across the flats and waterways, it is charming.

From Le Faou our path heads west and south to cross the neck of the land that divides the Le Faou estuary from that of the river Aulne. This is farming country now, full of small villages, and the walker will pass through several of these down to the banks of the Aulne, and up to the road bridge across the estuary, at Terenez. This backwater was once used to shelter warships of the French Reserve Fleet, and the old warriors may still be there, swinging with the tide on their rusty anchor chains.

The path leads across the bridge, past the Chapelle de Folgat, and into the fishing village of Landévennec, a very pretty place with adequate accommodation and the coast close by — a good place in which to pass the night.

Landévennec lies at the northern side of the

Above: **The castle of Fougères which is situated on the frontiers of Brittany.**

Right: **Crossing an improvised bridge in the Forêt de Rennes.**

Rivoal, from where the path descends to a stream, past a watermill and on to Kergombou, up and down to the St Rivoal stream, then contouring round a hill to another valley and into a thick wood, which the path traverses due west into the Cranou forest, always heading to the west, drawn on by the ever-approaching sea. From St Rivoal to the estuary at Le Faou is some 20 miles (32 km), a full day's walk, across the Monts d'Arrée, but easy going to the western edge of the great Parc Régional

beautiful Presqu'île de Crozon, one of our favourite areas of Brittany. Walkers with a few days to spare could not do better than to walk out to the tip of this 'almost island' to Roscanval or Morgat, or the beautiful atmospheric little port of Camaret. A couple of days wandering here would be delightful, especially if the weather is mild.

Back at Landévennec, the Tro-Breiz path cuts south, across the base of the peninsula, through woods and farmland to Argol, which has a very fine late Gothic church and a small calvary. Here the next range of 'mountains' begins, but again these are Breton mountains, rising to the peak of the Ménez-Hom at 1080ft (330m). The path climbs steadily to the top of this round, heath-covered hill for splendid views across to the roadstead of Brest, and then down a lane to the hamlet of Ste-Marie du Ménez Hom, which has a sixteenth-century calvary and a small chapel beside the road.

From Ste Marie, the GR path heads for the coast, leaving the 'Argoat' for the 'Armorica', and arrives eventually at La Lieue de Grève, a long beach, 3 miles (5 km) in length, snuggled back into the coastline just south of the Presqu'île de Crozon. Follow the path which runs behind the beach to the south, onto the village of Ste-Anne la Palud. This has a modern chapel and not much else, but there is plenty of accommodation a few miles away at Locronan. Locronan is a very fine, old-Breton town, built of glittering granite and full of good architecture, well worth a visit.

Next day, walk back, out of Locronan, down the minor road to Kervel, and pick up the path for one last day's walk down the beach, into the port of Douarnenez. Douarnenez is one of the great fishing ports of Brittany, a good spot to spend a few days walking on the local paths, or simply to end this journey.

Gentle walking through a Breton village.

The rolling Breton countryside in spring.

Introduction

Brittany has two great overriding advantages for the British walker. The climate is agreeable and it's not too far away. To be more precise, the Western province of Brittany, Finistère, which juts out into the Atlantic, does tend to be somewhat damp, but the southern province of the Morbihan, where this walk is set, is always drier than the rest, even in a rainy summer. This walk, across the Lanvaux moors, is not unlike a walk in Britain, on Exmoor perhaps, but as we shall see, there are some differences which justify including it here.

Historically and topographically, Brittany has always been divided into two distinct areas.

Firstly, there is the difference between the coast and the countryside, between *Armorica*, the 'land facing the sea', and the *Argoat*, the 'country of wood.' Secondly, and of growing social importance over the years, there is the division between the *'pays Breton'*, the Breton-speaking areas to the west, and the *'pays Gallo'*, the predominantly French-speaking areas to the east, close to the dread frontier with France. Today the Breton language is rarely heard outside Finistère, and although it is currently enjoying a brief revival, the decline in the use of Breton is probably irreversible. This walk, across the moorlands of the Landes de

Lanvaux, the GR38, is part of a longer footpath which will, when completed, link the bleak Pointe du Raz in Finistère with the valley of the river Loire far to the east. The Landes, which form this central section, straddle a long granite ridge, 42 miles (75km) long, and about 5 miles (8km) wide, between Baud in the west and the historic little town of Rochefort-en-Terre, from where the footpath runs south, out of the Landes, to Redon on the river Vilaine.

This is a very pleasant French walk and one that can be made at any time between late March and the end of October. In spring the slopes of the Landes are covered with flowers, the heather flames in October, and the golden broom is in bloom all the year round, which gives rise to the old French proverb that girls should only be kissed when the broom, (the *genêt)* is in flower, which means at any time.

Those walkers well used to rambling in Britain, will find the terrain of the Landes somewhat familiar, not unlike Exmoor or parts of Dartmoor. It can be wet underfoot and mud is not uncommon, so at least light boots and gaiters are advisable. Showers are not unknown in summer, so rainproof clothing should be carried, as should shorts, tee-shirt, and hat — when the sun *is* shining the Morbihan is hot.

Accommodation is not hard to find, with a number of *gîtes d'étape* available, run by the efficient ABRI organisation and there are plenty of small hotels and camp sites. Those who wish to camp wild can find plenty of *camping-à-la-ferme* pitches, and where these are not available the local farmers are usually willing to let a backpacker use the corner of a field without difficulty or payment.

Apart from the green countryside and the pleasant, fairly easy walking, the Morbihan is full of historic and prehistoric sites: castles, churches, megalithic remains. Do not leave the Morbihan without seeing some of these. A visit to the unique stone lines and menhirs of Carnac is almost essential on any visit to this part of France.

The Route

This walk, according to the *Topo-Guide,* begins with a section of the GR which lies west of Baud, from the lock at Menazen on the Nantes-Brest canal. From there the footpath follows the towpath to the village of Pont-Augan on the river Eval, at the point where it feeds yet another canal, the Canal of the river Blavet. This is a pretty spot, a pleasant place to start the walk, and a very different side of Brittany from that commonly found on the tourist-infested coast. Follow the path past the cross at Botcario, just south of the D3 road to Baud, and follow minor tracks south and west to Coët-Vin, on the outskirts of Baud and then turn south for Quinipily.

Quinipily is famous for its statue, a somewhat battered Greek or Roman relic of great antiquity, which stands in a kind of grotto behind

A raised track which takes walkers across the cultivated land.

a farmhouse just off the path. This is the *Vénus de Quinipily*. She has lived hereabouts for two thousand years or more and was probably erected by the Romans. When the Christian era began in Brittany the local priests took her to be a graven image and threw her into the river. The locals are fond of their Venus and they dredged her out again, and she has been in and out of the river many times in the last several hundred years. If she looks a little world-weary now, be compassionate; she has been through a lot.

The footpath crosses the Eval, and then passes through the woods by Quinipily, and then along the banks of a stream to the ruins of the castle of Cammorre, or Konomor, from where it leads on, close to the village of Camors, which lies a little off the path, with shops and hotels, a good place to spend the first night on the GR38.

From Camors the path continues south and east across the thick Forêt-de-Floranges, following forest rides and tracks. It is possible to cut much of this route, although it's an easy, enjoyable path, which runs past the menhir, or standing stone which marked the limits of the demesne of the Lords of Camors, and eventually to the stone lines or *alignements* at Cornevec, and the old Roman road to Loperhet, after which the path turns south for Porh Moro and the Chapel at St Meriadec, close to Notre-Dame-des-Pins, and the village of Bieuzy-Lanvaux, a picturesque and rather remote village on the western slopes of the Landes de Lanvaux. The ruined abbey here was built by the Cistercians (who liked remote places) in 1158. From there the path leads out to the Etang de la Forêt, where there is a camp site and a well-appointed ABRI *gîte*. These ABRI shelters are among the best in France, so do not forget to obtain an up-to-date list from ABRI (see appendix) before setting out.

After leaving the lake, the path climbs to give good views over the countryside and passes on to the pilgrim village of Loperhet, and the shrine of St Brigette. St Brigette was an Irish saint, of course, and one often invoked by local women who wish to have babies. The village is even more ancient for there was a pagan shrine here in the time of the Druids. The path follows the Landes east, but on the southern side of the

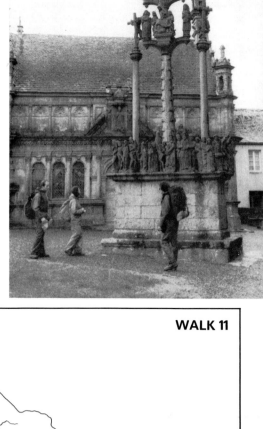

Right: A group of walkers stop to admire a Breton calvary.

Distance: 91 miles (154km).
Time Required: Two weeks.
Type of Walk: A moorland walk, suitable for well-equipped walkers or backpackers.
Maps and Guide: FFPR-CNSGR GR38 *Sentier des Landes de Lanvaux.* IGN *Carte Verte* Nos. 15 & 24. *Michelin Green Guide to Brittany. A Visitor's Guide to Brittany,* (Moorland Publishing).
Getting to the Start: By Brittany Ferry to St Malo and train or bus to Baud.

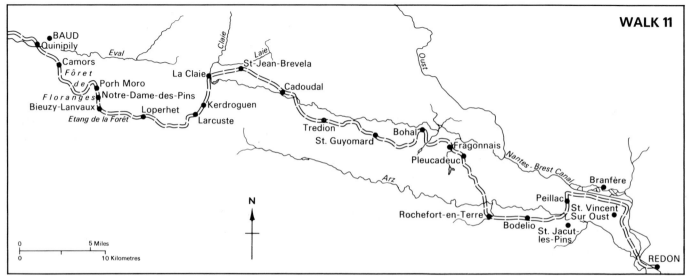

WALK 11

BAUD
Quinipily
Eval
Camors
Fôret
de
Floranges
Porh Moro
Notre-Dame-des-Pins
Bieuzy-Lanvaux
Loperhet
Etang de la Forêt
Kerdroguen
Larcuste
La Claie
Claie
Laie
St-Jean-Brevela
Cadoudal
Tredion
St. Guyomard
Bohal
Fragonnais
Pleucadeuc
Oust
Branfère
Peillac
Rochefort-en-Terre
Bodelio
St. Jacut-les-Pins
Arz
Nantes-Brest Canal
St. Vincent Sur Oust
REDON

N

0   5 Miles
0   10 Kilometres

main ridge, turning north to cross the main D767 road a little south of Colpo. Colpo is a good spot for lunch or even a night stop. Colpo was built, or rather rebuilt, by the Princess Bacciochi, a niece of Napoleon Bonaparte, in 1858, and she is buried in the village church.

From here the path plunges deeper into the past, through the excavated Neolithic remains at Min-Goh-Ru, near Larcuste, which date from around 4000 BC, and across the trace of another Roman road to the sixteenth-century Chapel at Kerdroguen. This part of the Landes is quite hilly, and well wooded, a secret little place, full of unexpected views, lonely farms, scattered hamlets, a place where good map reading can be helpful. The path arrives at La Claie on the river of the same name, which the path follows for some way along the banks before climbing again to the ridge and arriving in the village of St-Jean-Brevelay, where there is plenty of accommodation, including a good camp site.

St Jean lies on the northern edge of the Landes moors, between two river valleys, those of the Claie and the Laie. Here the walker gets a good glimpse of that mixture of the pagan and Christian which is common hereabouts. A huge pre-Christian menhir stands opposite the church, but St Jean is dedicated to an early British saint, whose relics were brought here in the tenth century by monks fleeing from the Vikings.

From St Jean, climb to the crest of the ridge, past a cross and follow the northern lip of the moor east, through a mixture of woodland and open country to the village of Cadoudal. Cadoudal was a centre for the Royalist, Catholic Chouans, who fought for the King after the Revolution of 1789, and in spite of considerable

Above: **The weather won't always be fine. Here a group of walkers, protected by hats and waterproofs, smile through the drizzle.**

Left: **A Breton menhir.**

oppression, were still waging a guerrilla war during the later days of the Napoleonic Empire.

Close by, just a few kilometres down the footpath lies the medieval castle of Tredion, once a hunting lodge used by the Dukes of Brittany while they were pursuing stags in the forests hereabouts. It stands on the edge of a lake, and the path runs round the lake and into the old village of Tredion, which dates from 1121. The villagers used to be ironworkers and charcoal burners, and it still looks like a working village, busy with its own affairs, not much interested in the walkers who pass by in the summer rain.

From Tredion the path goes east, through the woods, and then circles to the north, up towards the Claie again, to Chemara, and the Chapel of St Nicolas, and the so-called Grotto of the Wolves. The medieval village of Lesonnais is a curious, interesting place, with the usual menhirs dotted about here and there. A little to the north of the path lies the village of St Guyomard, which is a good place to visit with a small but very interesting museum of prehistory.

The path now crosses the centre of the Landes, in fairly open country, past another chapel dedicated to St Maurice and through the site of a Roman camp, in the valley of the Glouty, close to yet another vast menhir, the Pierre Longue, which stands just to the south of the track as it turns left for Bohal.

Bohal is a great centre for day walking, surrounded by waymarked footpaths, all indicated by blue flashes on the trees and rocks. The countryside here is delightful, fairly open and rolling, with pleasant views to the north and east. From here on, the GR3 seems to relax, wandering south and east to the farm at Fragonnais and skirting the village at Pleucadeuc, before zig-zagging south to one of the most delightful towns in all Brittany, Rochefort-en-Terre.

Rochefort stands above another river, the Arz, looking out north and west to the river gorges and the Lanvaux moors. The *Topo-Guide* tells us that Rochefort is a *petite cité de caractère*, and that the inhabitants are called the *Coucous*, which makes it all sound rather twee, but Rochefort is, in fact, an ancient and rather splendid place, an essential stop and well worth a day of anyone's time. There is plenty of accommodation, and the ruins of an ancient castle and a quite remarkable church, Notre-Dame-de-la-Tronchaye, are well worth seeing. This church contains among other treasures, one of the rare Black Virgins.

After a day in Rochefort, take up the trail again, heading due east, clinging to the top of the steep ridge above the Arz, to Bodelio, which has a huge, walled park, and past the restored windmills at La Balle and then off the path for a little way to the little village of St-Jacut-les-Pins, which is the perfect place for lunch.

Rejoin the path and descend the ridge to the north, to cross another lower ridge through Peillac, a pretty spot, and up to the banks of the Canal Nantes-à-Brest, and the river Oust. Follow the towpath to the east, to the Pont de Branfère, where another GR, the GR347 heads north to the great castle of the Rohans at Josselin.

Branfère is a rather splendid spot, quite remote and peaceful, if rather marshy. From here a track leads to Brecihan, and so to the Ile-aux-Pies, another splendid spot, where the river Oust breaks through the escarpment of the Landes, and heads south for the village of St Vincent sur Oust, which is graced by the nearby château at Boro. The footpath continues to follow or skirt the Canal Nantes-à-Brest, an easy, level route which, after another 6 miles (7km), arrives at Redon, and the end of this journey.

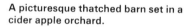

A picturesque thatched barn set in a cider apple orchard.

Walk 12 ACROSS THE ALPS

Introduction

The GR5 footpath (Sentier Hollande-Méditerranée) is a very long GR footpath, running right down the Alpine chain into the sea at Nice. Much of this path follows the great GTA, (Grande Traversée des Alpes) path, from Lake Geneva to the Mediterranean, a real outdoor adventure. From the village of St Dalmas-Valblore, the GR52, a *variante* which is now an established footpath in its own right, swerves off the main route through the Parc de Mercantour and the Vallée des Merveilles, and reaches the sea at Menton. This walk, however, follows the direct GR5 south from the Col de Larche in Haute-Provence, a fairly short but still demanding high-mountain walk, the ideal two-week trip for fit, committed backpackers or hill walkers. In early June snow will still be found in the cols and so an ice axe, crampons, and the ability to use them, might well be necessary. In summer it will certainly be hot but the altitude and the possibility of mist and summer storms means that some windproof clothing is essential. It can be very cold at night, with ice on the rocks in the morning. Snow will arrive on the

The Alpine rivers and streams can be fast flowing and cold. They have to be crossed with care.

Distance: 97 miles (154km)

Type of Walk: A high mountain walk requiring fitness, some experience and full hill walking equipment.

Time Required: Two weeks.

Season: Late spring to early autumn.

Maps and Guides: FFPR-CNSGR Guide GR5-52 *Col de Larche to Nice.* IGN *Carte Verte* No. 195. Didier-et-Richard maps, *Alpes de Provence* and *Haut-Pays Niçois.*

Getting to the Start: By train and bus north from Nice.

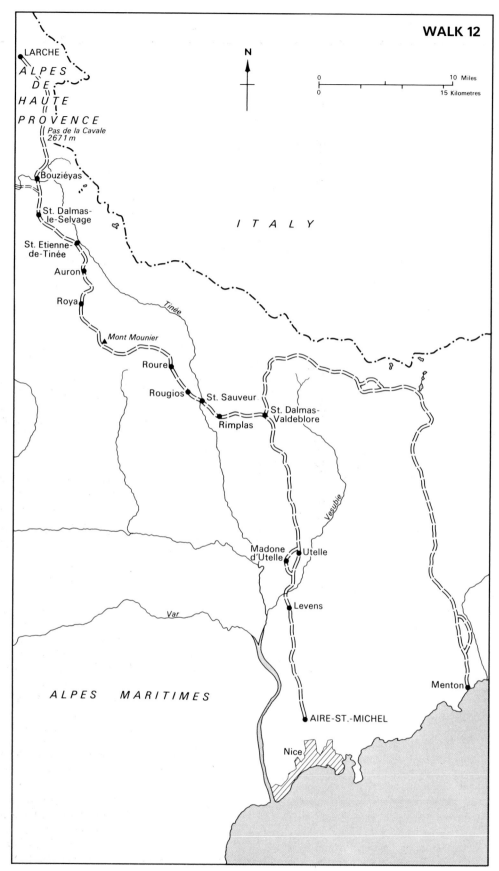

tops by early October and this walk should not be attempted before mid-June at the earliest and is probably not worth contemplating after mid-October in a normal year.

The accommodation varies. Mountain huts, *gîtes* and tents will provide the bulk of the shelter, but small Alpine villages come along at decent intervals to provide the walker with a little rest and a filling meal.

The Route

This walk begins at Larche, 5430ft (1655m), a high mountain village which was destroyed by the Germans in 1944. The modern reconstruction is a little short on charm, although the mountain setting is quite spectacular. From here, the path climbs beside the Ubayette, passing the Col de Larche to the east, to Port Rouge, 6255ft (1907m), and into the Lauzanier valley. This is climbers' country with plenty of huts and shelters dotted about, and the path follows the *vallon* to the Lac du Lauzanier at 7490ft (2284m). This is a beautiful spot with plenty of tent pitches available. From the lake the path climbs steadily to the Pas de la Cavale, 8760ft (2671m), which is the first landmark on the journey and at this point the walker passes from the Alpes de Haute-Provence to the Alpes-Maritimes.

On the steep south side of the col, the path zig-zags down to a group of little lakes at 7685ft (2343m), and eventually to Salse Morène. To get this far on the trail will take even a fit walker

most of the first day, so camping here or further back at Lauzanier would be advisable. Those who require accommodation in a hotel or *gîte* must press on to Bouziéyas, another two hours' walk, over yet another col, the Col des Fourdes, 7420ft (2262m). Bouziéyas has a small *gîte*, organised by the GTA organisation. Apart from this, there is only one small hotel, so pre-booking is advisable.

At Bouziéyas the walker has descended to 6175ft (1883m) and must begin again with another long climb to the Col de la Colombière at 7340ft (2237m) a splendid spot where the GR56, the *Tour de l'Ubaye* footpath meets the GR5. Those who are very fit or with time in hand, can climb still higher to the east, up to the top of the Tête de Vinaigre at 7340ft (2394m), for a fine view over this magnificent mountain country, but do not consider leaving the main path in times of mist or low cloud. From the col it is a two-hour steep descent to the village of St Dalmas-le-Selvage, another attractive mountain village, and one well used to walkers, so a good place for lunch or a night stop.

Mountain walkers will now know the daily routine of such a walk. It consists of the climb to the col, which may be more or less difficult, depending on the steepness of the path and the weather, a rest at the top, then the long descent to the village in the next valley. The next col, the Col d'Anelle, lies at 5705ft (1739m), and the next village, St Etienne-de-Tinée, at 3750ft (1144m). St Etienne is a popular walking centre

Top left: **Footpaths often follow alongside rivers in the valley bottoms. Not all Alpine walks follow the crest.**

Top: **This was taken in January. Two weeks later everything was back under snow again.**

Above: **Wild camping in the scenic foothills of the Alps is a delight.**

in summer and at weekends, when walkers, mostly members of local FFRP groups, flock up here from the Côte d'Azur and Nice. St Etienne has plenty of hotels and restaurants where those who feel like a day off from the GR5 could pass a pleasant day and night.

From here it is no great distance to Auron, which at 5255ft (1602m) is another popular walking centre, although now rather better known as a downhill ski resort. It is possible to take the cable car up to the top station, which gives a fine view and saves another slog, and rejoin the GR5 by walking east along the ridge to the Col du Blainon at 6595ft (2011m).

This col looks down to the southern Roya valley and to the village of Roya at the head of the valley, another popular spot for walkers and climbers. There is a *gîte d'étape* (GTA) and a small hotel here, so it is possible to stop a night before setting out on the next stage of the journey with another long, full morning climb to the Col de Crousette at 8135ft (2480m). It would be a good idea to quit the path here and walk along the ridge to the north, to the CAF hut on Mont Mounier, and then up to the top, for yet more marvellous views. On a clear day (and this diversion should not be attempted otherwise), there are views to the Mediterranean, even to distant Corsica if you are lucky, and certainly to a vast range of nearby peaks in France and Italy.

Back at the col, the path continues, contouring now to the east, circling and descending slowly to the Col de Mulines at 6500ft (1982m). This is fairly wild country and the waymarks are few and far between, so good map reading will be helpful as the path continues to the Vacherie de Roure, following a torrent for much of the way. There is a *gîte d'étape* at Roure, and from here the path continues beside the stream to Rougios, an alpine plateau, littered with barns, a pleasant open spot after this long scramble down the mountainside.

An hour further away, and even lower down at 3595ft (1096m), the path enters Roure, a curious, half-empty village, with a *gîte,* a shop-cum-café, and some very friendly inhabitants. From here the path descends in zig-zags, crossing the road in several places until it arrives at last in St Sauveur-sur-Tinée, the lowest point on the journey so far, at only 1625ft (496m). The steep descent is very hard on the legs, especially the legs of those under heavy packs, and a night-stop here will be welcome.

Compared with the places we have passed so far, St Sauveur is a metropolis. There are hotels, restaurants, shops, everything in plural, and all in a delightful old stone setting. After a night in

St Sauveur, the next place on the path, Rimplas, is something of a shock, being twice as high at 3330ft (1016m), but almost empty of people. From here the path goes east, often in sight of the road that climbs steadily, as the path does, to the pretty, bustling little village of St Dalmas-Valdeblore. There are actually two villages here, though they have now grown together. Here again, this is a popular centre for walkers but those on the GR5, or especially on the GTA are welcome and clearly regarded as heroes.

The walker has a choice here, for the GR52 path diverts away, heading for the sea at Menton, and passing through the new Parc de Mercantour and past the prehistoric rock carvings of the Vallée des Merveilles. This is a route of some 62 miles (100km) and will take a fit walker about a week — but it is very beautiful and well worth considering.

Our path continues down the GR5, switchbacking over still more cols, the Col de Varaire, 5610ft (1710m), the Col du Caire Gros, 6250ft (1906m), and several more, all close to the 6560-ft (2000-m) mark, a testing section of the way. There is no accommodation or subsistence available from St Dalmas-Valdeblore until Utelle, which is a very full day's walk, listed as nearly six hours in the *Topo-Guide*. As it lies over a continuous succession of cols, nine hours might be nearer the mark. Those with tents, or those prepared to bivouac, may prefer to stop at Maison Forestière, a very pleasant spot. Otherwise, leave St Dalmas early in the day and march steadily, trying to avoid spending too much time on the views. On balance, a camp at Maison Forestière, would be the best solution, and make this section less of a chore and much more enjoyable.

Utelle is a pleasant little town, quite large, and well worth a night stop. It stands on a ridge overlooking the Vésubie, and has plenty of accommodation, and an exquisite little church dedicated to St Veran. Those who arrive here early or who still have energy to spare can spend the afternoon walking the circular *variante* to the Col d'Ambellard, and visiting the sanctuary of the Madonna of Utelle. This stands at 3850ft (1174m), and offers one of the finest viewpoints over the Alpes-Maritimes.

The path from Utelle follows this *variante* for a little distance to the Chapelle St-Antoine, before swooping down abruptly to the D67, and climbing equally swiftly to the village of Levens, a good place for lunch. From now on the path runs through the lower and more populated foothills of the Alpes-Maritimes, through a number of pretty villages or hill towns, any one of which is worth stopping in for the night before a final morning's walk takes the traveller

to the Aire-St-Michel, and the end of this journey. From here, Nice is only minutes away by bus.

After the peace and quiet of the mountains, a sudden return to the noise and crowds of the Côte d'Azur can be shattering, so either leave quickly or return to St Dalmas, and take up that other Alpine path, the GR52, for another walk in the high and lonely hills, through Mercantour and the Valley of Marvels and so back to the coast at Menton.

Opposite page, top: **Walking down paths of loose shale such as this one in the Oissans Parc in Provence, requires care if you are not to slip.**

Opposite page, bottom: **A group of well-equipped walkers pause to quench their thirst in the high Alps.**

Above: **The dramatic scenery of the high Alps.**

Walk 13 A WALK IN THE VELAY

Above: **Taking advantage of a farm track across the Velay.**

Opposite page, left: **A little village nestles in the green hills of the Velay.**

Opposite page, top: **A walker enjoying the 'countryside of the wide horizons'.**

Opposite page, middle: **Towpaths make good level trails.**

Opposite page, bottom: **The scenery in the Velay is a mixture of moorland, farm and forest which makes for stimulating walking.**

Introduction

This attractive route traverses a hilly region of the Auvergne, including the Monts du Velay, the Massif du Mézenc and the Massif du Meygal. At their most demanding, the gradients may prove tiring to the novice walker but they are hardly strenuous and never difficult. The only real word of warning is to watch out for the north-east slope of the Meygal, which can be very slippery when wet.

The only real restriction to walking in the Velay is snow, and since the cover may extend over a long period of time, often from December to April, this effectively rules out winter walking. At this time of the year the Velay belongs to the cross-country skier. To be sure of firmer ground, wait until the muddy conse-quences of the thaw have eased, around the middle or the end of May, and try to fit your walk in before the beginning of November.

Go prepared for a wide repertoire of weather at any time, including cold, wind and rain. The ground can also be rough in some parts, muddy in others, so a good pair of lightweight boots will be needed, and a compass will be useful.

The Velay, like much of the Auvergne, is often referred to as a 'gift of the volcanoes' and a 'museum of the fires of the earth', since both owe much of their visible geography to their igneous roots. For British walkers, the GR40, a 100-mile (160-km) circuit which in parts follows a line of old eruptions and both skirts and defines the broad plateau of the Velay, offers views that cannot be found on our home island.

The Velay is known locally as the

'countryside of the wide horizons' and the 'land without barriers'. The only major interruption to the sea of green meadows or the blanketing of pine trees is the valley of the Loire. Best known for its broad, gentle sweep through the châteaux country, France's grandest river spends its infancy running north-south through the heart of the Velay, which supplies the name for the local *département:* Haute-Loire.

The Velay region is famed among French walking enthusiasts, not only for the inspiring, expansive scenery, but also for the criss-cross of ancient routes. The GR40 in part follows stretches of *draille* road along which cattle were herded to market, along the routes trodden by Roman soldiers and the commercial arteries employed by salesmen of the Middle Ages, carrying their pack-horse wares from one market town to the next.

Although the GR40 is a trail that circles around Le Puy, most walkers will visit the town itself, either as an obvious link to transport home, or as a place to spend a couple of days pottering about. Situated on the Loire, Le Puy's most distinguishing landmarks are the ancient volcanic 'puys' or plugs of rock, one capped by an eleventh-century Romanesque chapel, and the other, the even higher Rocher Corneille, crowned by an enormous rust-red statue of Notre-Dame-de-France and the baby Jesus, made from more than two hundred cannons

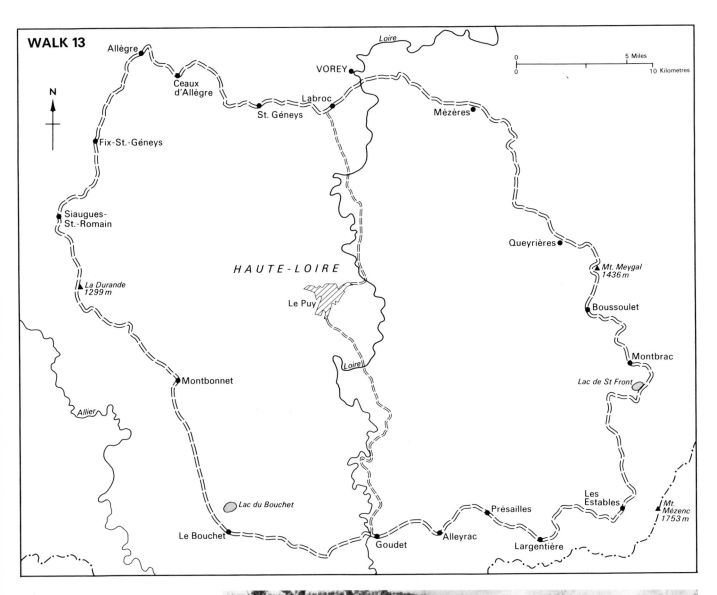

WALK 13

N

Allègre
Ceaux d'Allègre
St. Géneys
Labroc
Loire
VOREY
Mézères

Fix-St.-Géneys

Siaugues-St.-Romain

HAUTE-LOIRE

Queyrières

▲ Mt. Meygal
1436 m

Boussoulet

▲ *La Durande*
1299 m

Le Puy

Montbrac

Lac de St Front

Montbonnet

Allier

Loire

Lac du Bouchet

Les Estables

▲ Mt. Mézenc
1753 m

Présailles

Le Bouchet

Goudet
Alleyrac
Largentière

0 ___ 5 Miles
0 ___ 10 Kilometres

Distance: 100 miles (160km).
Time required: One to two weeks.
Type of walk: A fairly gentle circular hill walk through the hills of the Auvergne around Le Puy.
Maps and Guides: FFRP-CNSGR *Topo-Guide* GR40, *Tour du Velay. Portrait of the Auvergne* by Peter Graham, (Hale). IGN *Carte Verte* No. 5.
Getting to the Start: By train from Paris, Lyon or Le Puy.

Cattle still pull the plough in the Velay.

captured from the Russians at Sebastopol in the Crimean War.

The Route

After a day in Le Puy, seeing all the sights, the walker is offered a choice of walks out to the circling GR40, on a number of interesting trails, the GR3, a number of local footpaths, or by bus or train.

Vorey, 12 miles (20km) north of Le Puy, with its rail station, hotels, shops and restaurants, makes the most convenient starting point for this walk through the Velay and is also the most symbolic place to both begin and end the trip, since the river Loire slices through the GR40 just to the south of the town. Those who walk all the way here from Le Puy along the GR3, will meet the GR40 to the west of Vorey just outside the hamlet of Labroc. Soon afterwards, leave the minor road and tackle the first of the uphill gradients which will take the walker through forested countryside, a landscape that will become familiar during the next few days. There is also a stretch of path here which is curiously called the 'route of the unemployed', since it was used frequently during World War II by jobless refugees.

The path barely touches the old fortified village of Saint-Geneys and its ancient crater landscape, before leading along a minor road for a short spell into a cross-country section, through Anviac and on northwards through the woods of Redon and Reyrat and on down to Ceaux d'Allègre. This makes a good first night stop, leaving you fresh for the next morning, which begins with a climb up Mont Bar, (hardly Mont Blanc but it does offer some grand views across the Velay, especially if you opt for the *variante* path to the lake-filled crater summit). Mont Bar, as you will readily recognise, is a volcano of the classic 'stromboli' type, and according to legend, you only have to throw a tiny stone into the lake and all hell will be let loose!

The next stretch, from Allègre, parallels the D40 road as far as Mentéyres and then carries on across a mixture of open countryside and forest. At Fix-St-Geneys, so called because it marks the frontier between the Auvergne and the Velay, the GR40 and GR41, which have so far run in unison, part company, the former accompanying the D4 as far as the remarkably-named village of Pisseboeuf. From here the walker passes through an enormous volcanic depression called the crater of Chantuzier, named after a tiny hamlet on the southern fringe.

At Siaugues-St-Romain the GR40 passes the thirteenth-century château of Saint-Romain, which once belonged to the Lafayette family. After a steady climb the walker will be rewarded with some fine views across the valley of the river Allier on the right, and further south the spectacular 'maar' volcanic depression known as the 'Marnis de Limagne'. After a further climb the 4260-ft (1299-m) summit of the Durande is reached, which also marks a border between the Velay and the Auvergne. The view is tremendous.

The dramatic site of the church of St. Michel de l'Aiguille, at Le Puy.

Villages shelter under the rim of the saucer-shaped Velay.

in 1878 and described the river as '... a limpid stream, like crystal'. You must cross the river here, at the half-way stage of the route, and if time is short you may cut back to Le Puy on the GR3 which leaves the GR40 just outside the town. Those who choose to press on must not feel daunted by the steep climb up the granite sides of the valley, the Côte de l'Ayre, to Fugères and Alleyrac.

The next points of specific geographic interest are the twin Monts Breysse, surrounded by the ancient woods which were once the lair of highwaymen waiting to pounce on unwary travellers on the Roman road which led to the Rhône Valley. Some historians have argued that the route between Présailles and Le Beage, known as The Roman Way (as distinct from *a* Roman way, of which there are many) may well form part of a famous 'route du Pal' which traversed the Massif Central and was the principal and probably only link between Provence in the south and Brittany in the distant west. Follow this track as far as Largentière and then turn east and north, passing through the ancient forest of Clergeat and on to Les Etables, the highest community in the Massif and an important winter cross-country ski resort.

Mont Mézenc, whose summit, or summits, can be reached after one-and-a-half hours, lies to the east of the GR40 at 5750ft (1753m), the northernmost point of the Cévennes, while a little to the north stands Mont d'Alambre. The route then follows an old *draille* or drovers' road which once carried cattle between the Cévennes and the Languedoc. Beyond is another of the typical maars of the region, the Lac St-Front. Beyond the villages of Roffiac (the second highest village of the Velay after Les Etables), Montbrac and Boussoulet, the GR40 passes the enormous forest and then proceeds on over the 4710-ft (1436-m) summit of Meygal. The walker then follows the pretty Combenoire valley to Queyrières and into still more deep forest.

The last leg of the journey is the busiest section, in the sense that it passes through a higher density of villages than before, and there are more stretches of road walking, though they are all very minor roads and do not detract from the rural ambience. Of particular interest is a 'Le Puy'-type chapel, perched on the top of a volcanic plug at Glavenas, the pretty village of Blanlhac, several patches of lush valley and forest scenery, and finally to the friendly face of the Loire at Vorey and the end of this beautiful walk.

One of the most interesting sections along the entire route lies immediately to the south of the lovely village of Montbonnet. Not only does it lead you along the tracks of an ancient Roman road, built by Agrippa to link Lyon and Toulouse, but the contrasting scenery of open landscapes to the right and steep-sided woods on the left make a stimulating change from the closed woods and open horizon combinations experienced so far.

It is worth leaving the Roman road just to the south of Mont Recours to follow a *variante* to Lac du Bouchet, which lies on the Robert Louis Stevenson Trail and which occupies an enormous volcanic crater surrounded by forests, to see the Cross of the Goat, commemorating the legendary survivors of a flood which wiped out an entire village that had refused to give hospitality to a poor beggar — all except for one old lady and her pet goat. Legend has it that you can still hear the sound of the church bell rising from the bottom of the lake on a still night. Further on, beyond the village of Le Bouchet, you will also pass the maar of Costaros, another crater scar. This half-mile wide depression or 'maar' is dry in all but times of heavy rain. From here the path leads on to Goudet.

Goudet is an attractive place to pass the night, or even to spend a rest day. Apart from the back-up facilities of hotel, camp site, restaurants, bars and a weekly market, it is delightfully situated on the banks of the Loire in a pretty green valley with the ruins of a fourteenth century château to lend a focal point to your visit. Robert Louis Stevenson came here

Walk 14 A TOUR OF THE VIVARAIS

Introduction

France is a country with many faces and not all of them are familiar, even to the people of France. Parts of the country have suffered massive depopulation since the last war, creating areas full of fine scenery but empty of people, and one of these depopulated areas is the Vivarais. The name *Vivarais* dates back to before the Revolution of 1792, to the days of the *Ancien Régime*. Today, it is better known as the Ardèche, a region of high hills, deep ravines, rushing streams, and as the birthplace of great rivers. The Loire rises here, on the slopes of the Gerbier de Jonc, and this region contains the great watershed of France, where some rivers flow north-west to the Atlantic and others south towards the Mediterranean.

This path, the GR420, *Tour du Haut-Vivarais,* is a composite footpath, and not an original creation. It is made up of sections of the GR7, 73, 427, 42 and 421, all linked into a long, superb, circular footpath, which enters the Vivarais from the western bank of the Rhône to the slopes of Mont Mézenc far to the west, and will take the walker through some of the finest and least-known hill country of France.

The countryside is wild and rough, rising to 4600ft (1500m) at the Mézenc, falling to around 1640ft (500m) by the Rhône. This far south it will be very hot in summer, but the weather at any time can tend to be dramatic, with deep snow and blizzards in winter, and high winds, storms and lightning in summer. The path itself is not over-demanding but the walker attempting it should be fit, experienced and well-equipped.

Unless the seasons are unusually extreme, it should be possible to complete this walk at any time between April and September, with the spring and autumn as the best choice, avoiding the high, hot days of summer. The spring flowers and the autumn colours are the two great attractions which should be seen if possible.

There is an adequate, if not abundant, amount of accommodation on the way, in small hotels, *auberges* and *gîtes d'étape,* but camping

Distance: 125 miles (208km).
Time required: Two or three weeks.
Type of walk: Through the hill-walking country of the Midi, a trip suitable for fit walkers and backpackers
Maps and Guides: FFRP-CNSGR Guide GR420, *Tour du Haut Vivarais.* IGN *Carte Verte* Nos. 50 and 52.
Getting to the Start: By rail to Tournon, Valence or Le Puy, then bus to St Péray, St Bonnet or Les Estables.

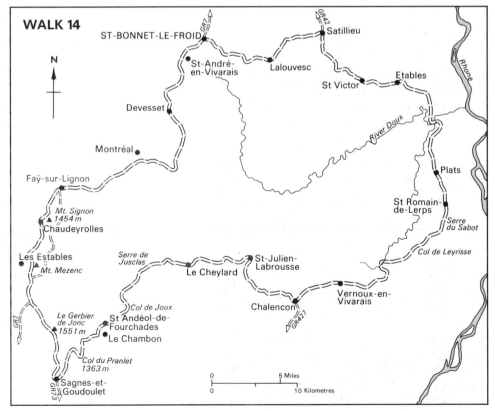

or bivouacking may be necessary to cut short some long stages. This walk combines a challenge, with the thrill of crossing a part of France which most walkers have still to discover, and we commend it to your serious consideration.

The Route

This walk begins in the little village of St-Bonnet-le-Froid, which lies in the north of the Ardèche. It begins with a climb out of the village onto a ridge, and then south, skirting and crossing the local D9 road. This is also the route of the GR7 footpath, which the GR420 follows for a considerable distance across country which rises to the 3280-ft (1000-m) mark, passing to the west of St-André-en-Vivarais, a pretty place which is well worth a coffee stop. In the late spring this is a delightful spot, the fields are full of flowers, the ground is often still marshy from the recent snow-melt. To the west again, a short distance off the GR, lies the château of Montrivert, set in the rising hills, a most attractive introduction to the Vivarais. The path carries on, contouring the hillsides to Louveton and, leaving the steeper slopes to the east, carries on south to Devesset. This village is also well worth a stop, for the footpath runs directly under the remains of an old *château-fort,* once a *commanderie* of the Knights of St John. Only one tower remains intact, but the site is magnificent. Past the dam at Pioullouse, the path enters Maisonneuve, actually quite ancient, with deep woodlands coming in from the east, and continues across hilly country, to the plateau and St Agrève.

St Agrève surrounds a little hill which is well worth climbing for the views from the top display many parts of the Ardèche and the valley of the river Reche. St Agrève would be a good place for a night stop, for there is plenty of accommodation and at least one good restaurant.

From St Agrève the track turns west and north, advancing steadily into the volcanic

Top: **The countryside can become tinder-dry in the hot summers. This fire-blasted slope reminds walkers to take care with fires.**

Middle: **The lush greenness of the Vivarais.**

Bottom: **The church of St. Sauveur.**

Opposite page, top: **A goat herd knits as she watches over her flock.**

Opposite page, bottom: **An ageing population and a crumbling farmhouse mark the drift of the young to the towns.**

country that surrounds the high peak of Mont Mézenc. Round, cut-topped hills, the relics of extinct volcanoes, now begin to appear, and the countryside becomes increasingly dramatic. The path continues to rise and fall, although the countryside remains above the 3280-ft (1000-m) mark, the route paralleling the D21, leaving Montréal to one side, and then arriving at Les Gueyts. Montréal is well worth a diversion, and the hill behind, at 3635ft (1108m), is worth climbing for more fine scenery is spread out below.

Those who camp could do well by pitching here for a day, for the countryside is beautiful, and there are unusual things to see hereabouts. South of Les Gueyts and easily reached on a

A party of French children set out on another day of their walking holiday.

footpath, lies the ruined, abandoned village of St Romain, while ahead the open country of the Velay approaches. The plateau of St Agrève is surrounded by a mixture of valleys and high plateaux, all worth inspection, before passing on to the cross-roads at Petit Freydier, out on a minor road into Hugons and open country, and moving from the Ardèche into the Haute-Loire *département*. Ahead lies a high part of the path and the stone cross of Vieille-Eglise, which can be seen from far away across the open country.

The next section, from Le Croix to Faÿ-sur-Lignon, is short but very interesting, only 3 miles (5km) through Vastres, a scattered hamlet with a fine little church, then across the river Lignon and up the slope into Faÿ, a considerable little town where the GR73 heads off for the South. Faÿ has several hotels and would be another good night-stop.

Leaving Faÿ, the path follows the road south for a short distance, to Le Pont-du-Mont, over rolling countryside, studded with high round hills, quite spectacular, and many of them higher now at 1590ft (1400m) or more, then around the western slopes of Mont Signon 4770ft (1454m), into Chaudeyrolles. The views from here are again superb, south across this country of the Vivarais to the alluring outline of Mont Mézenc at 5750ft (1753m). I can't think of a finer view in France. The path out of Chaudeyrolles runs right towards it, winding past waterfalls, through rocky outcrops and clumps of trees to the Croix de Peccata. From here the road and various footpaths run into the town of Les Estables, but our path heads up to the peak of the Mézenc.

Les Estables is a cross-country ski resort in winter, and a centre for walking in summer. First though, the path climbs to Mont Mézenc, for a look around the countryside, to the nearer volcanoes, and to the Gerbier de Jonc, the next major mountain. There is a *gîte* by the Croix de Peccata but most walkers will go on into Les Estables, before rejoining the route down the D631 at the Croix de Boutières, where the GR73 rejoins as well. The path heads south now, for the Col de la Clède and the Croix de Montouse, where the GR7 *variante* veers right, but we continue rising steadily to the Gerbier de Jonc at 5090ft (1551m). This is a stony, steep-sided cone, where the Loire begins as a mere trickle of water, flowing from the side of the scree. The climb to the top is worth it, with more of those volcanic hills appearing ahead and to the west. It's a spectacular spot, with views unmatched by anything else in France outside the Alps.

Once off the Gerbier, our path follows the road south for a while, along a traffic-filled route in summer, until just east of the hill at Les Coux, where a path climbs away to the west, round the slopes of the mountain and down to the village of Sagnes-et-Goudoulet, with the last section down the road into the village.

Sagnes marks the southern limit of this walk, but it is still less than half-way round the complete circuit. However, any walker who has come this far will now be fit, and can increase the pace if needs be.

A well-marked track runs north from Sagnes, towards a small col, and then along a drove road that follows a ridge up again to the watershed, from where some streams flow to the Atlantic and others to the Mediterranean. We head directly to the peak of the Suc d'Ourseyre, a spot surrounded by pine woods. The path skirts the crest down to the Col du Pranlet, where it follows the road for a few score metres and plunges north again, into some very wild and deserted country, past the ruins of Borne and the Col de Pranlet, 4470ft (1363m), then around and over various ridges into the forest of La Faye, down the ridge into St Andéol-de-Fourchades. St Andéol was once a marching camp for the legions of Caesar, and it is still clearly a fortress village, with the ruins of a medieval castle overlooking the half-deserted houses. The massive depopulation that has reduced the population of Central France has left St Andéol practically empty. Do not rely on stocking up with food here, but descend into the valley, to Le Chambon if necessary, before pressing on to the Col de Joux and following this ridge east and north to Cornuscle. We are now on the GR427. This route is easy to follow with close rising country to the right, and more open country falling away to the left. The GR path stays more or less along the ridge.

Cornuscle is an attractive mountain village, with houses littered over the hillside. From here the route continues, still on the ridge, a marvellous path to the Serre de Jusclas at 3280ft (1000m), through pine forest and open hill pasture, to the tip of La Berche and down the track into Brion.

According to the history books, Brion was once a seat of the powerful Lords of Cheylard, and it looks like it, a small, secure mountain hamlet from which the path descends rapidly into Cheylard, which is quite a large town, with camp sites and hotels, a good place to rest in for a day. The countryside hereabouts is steep, with wooded hillsides, and the path out follows the valley east to Francon, until the hill-climbing starts again, to St Julien Labrousse, and then a long, slow and winding descent to the small hamlet of Le Serre. Le Serre is very small, so press on across the delightful little river Glo for

Rob Hunter stands at the main watershed of France from where streams flow to the left to the Mediterranean and right to the Atlantic.

3 miles (5km) to Chalencon, which has a camp site and, by now, a *gîte*. There is the inevitable ruined castle, and the path out descends to the river, up to a farm and into Belay, from which it is only a short distance to one of the main halts on this footpath, the town of Vernoux-en-Vivarais, a splendid town. Stay a day in Vernoux, and enjoy the beautiful countryside, and take a rest among the old houses.

Following the path to the north, the walker soon comes into rough country, with steep hillsides curving down across the path from the south-east, as it descends the ridge towards the Col de Leyrisse on the D-road.

From here the path continues due north, skirting the country of Champis over the Serre du Sabot, still on the ridge, but descending slowly to St Romain-de-Lerps. The GR420 is now on the GR42, and arrows north again through wild, deserted country to Plats, which is very small, across the road which comes up from the east, and on to the hill above the valley of the Duzon. This again is spectacular country, steep and rugged once off the ridge. The path descends steeply to the Pont de Duzon, crosses the river Doux further up, and climbs again up the steep side along the left bank, again onto the crest and settles on the route to the north, into the village of Etables.

Etables lies at the base of a spur, which the path crosses to the west and descends again before circling another hill into the small town of St Victor. From here it is a comfortable two-day walk to the end of the tour at St Bonnet,

Left: **Lightweight footwear, shorts and T shirts are *de rigueur* on summer expeditions.**

Right: **The river Ardèche that runs through the Vivarais.**

across country which is, if that were possible, even lovelier and just as varied as anything we have seen so far. The contours become more gentle, the path follows them and the views expand step by step.

The path descends to the open valley at Satillieu, by the stream at Couranne, and clumbs to Huguet, back to *another* ridge and then across sweeping country to Lalouvesc, a fair-sized town which lies to the north of Mont Besset. From here it is a good but short day's walk over the last hill to Préaux, and so at last to St-Bonnet-le-Froid.

This is a marvellous walk which, as you can see from this brief description and a look at the map, involves a lot of ridge walking. It is a beautiful trip which should not be rushed so, if possible, allow three weeks for the journey.

Walk 15 ACROSS THE DORDOGNE

Introduction

The GR36 is one of the longer long-distance footpaths and runs the entire length of France, south into the Pyrénées. This section, from prehistoric Les Eyzies to the fortress city of Cahors, will give the walker a taste for the GR36, but more importantly, show a cross-section of the Dordogne, a region of France that has become increasingly popular with the British over the last twenty years. The Dordogne forms part of the old Duchy of Aquitaine, which the Plantagenets ruled until they were defeated at Castillion in the Dordogne in 1453. Even to the casual eye the classic attractions of the Dordogne are not hard to discover. This is a beautiful and historic part of France, full of fine towns and quaint villages, with some beautiful countryside and an agreeable climate. It has

been very popular with British visitors for the best part of three decades, but it is fair to say that not too many have travelled about there on foot.

Over those decades, the local footpath network has expanded considerably, and the Dordogne *département* is now full of good walks. Since this one, from Les Eyzies to Cahors, is fairly short, it might be an idea to spend a week exploring the other parts of the river valley on foot, cycle or by bus, before setting off on this trip, north to south across the *département* from the Vézère to the Lot.

This is truly a classic walk because it takes the traveller from the centre of prehistory, at Les Eyzies, probably after a visit to the caves at Lascaux II further up the valley, then south past

Footpaths often pass through private property. Here David Wickers and companion pass through Pechboutier Farm in the Dordogne.

Distance: 80 miles (130km)

Time Required: One week.

Terrain: A pleasant walk across rolling fields with some steeper sections.

Maps and Guides: FFPR *Topo-Guide* No. GR36 *Les Eyzies to Cahors. A Visitor's Guide to the Dordogne.* (Moorland Publishing). IGN 1:100,000 Nos. 40, 47, 48.

Getting to the Start: By train via Paris to Périgueux.

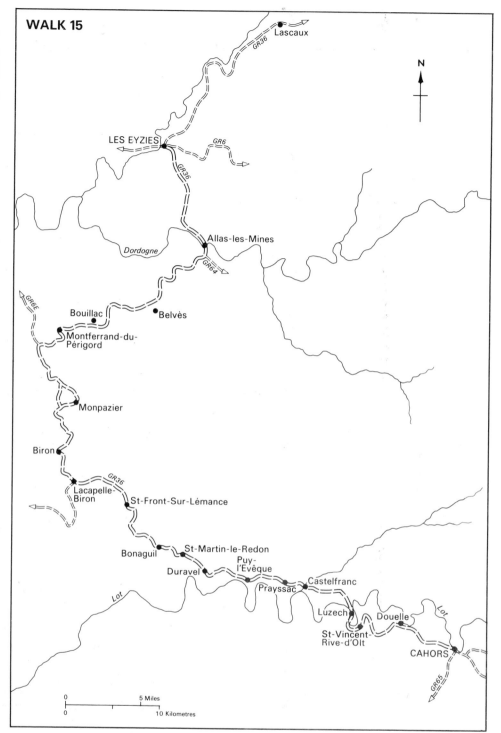

the great castle at Bonaguil, and finally on to the famous Pont Valentré at Cahors on the Lot, a splendid spot to end this short but classic walk.

This trip can be made at any time of the year, although boots and gaiters may be useful in the spring and autumn when the rains may make the paths muddy. It can be very hot, and quite difficult to find accommodation in July, August and early September, so if possible walk outside those months, perhaps at Easter or in the early autumn, when the weather is mild and the crowds absent.

This walk can be made by all kinds of walker, from the day-walker to the all-out backpacker, but will probably appeal most to those who love history.

The Route

This walk begins in the popular, if rather straggling, village of Les Eyzies-de-Tayac in the Vézère valley. A day in Les Eyzies would be advisable, to see the Prehistory Museum and the various local grottoes, some with cave paintings or carvings, although none is as elaborate as the famous Lascaux caves at Montignac. The Lascaux caves are now closed to the public, but a replica, Lascaux II, is open and well worth visiting. Les Eyzies has plenty of accommodation, from hotels to camp sites, and from here the GR strikes south, occupying the same route as the GR64 for the first stage of the journey.

Follow the waymarks to the Sarlat road and then turn off onto a dual track, up onto a ridge, and the top of Pech-Bertrou — *pech* being the local word for a spur or hill. The path kinks here, to follow the main track, and it is possible to swing off and visit the prehistoric grotto of La Mouthe, just half an hour off the route and a worthwhile diversion.

The countryside is hilly, not high but fairly steep, and well wooded. The path leads up to the village of Pech-Bertrou before descending into more open country and heading south into the town of St Cyprian, on the north bank of the

Youngsters pore over a map outside a village town hall.

Dordogne. St Cyprian is a medieval town, the place for a coffee stop before following the path east, across the flood plain of the Dordogne, crossing the river and turning into Allas-les-Mines, just in time for lunch.

Here the GR64 veers off the GR36, heading for the *bastide* town of Domme, a few kilometres away, a place which all visitors to the Dordogne ought to see, and walkers should certainly not miss. Returning to Allas, pick up the GR36 and climb out of the valley onto the south slopes and through the woods, turning south and then west, along the crest of a valley to La Plane.

The path descends into another valley and wanders south and west, through a number of small hamlets and villages, across the little Nauze, into the village of Fongauffier. There are good views in all directions hereabouts, and the path moves on, through Tournguil, or Tournhill, into the *bastide* town of Belvès, built by the English in the mid-fourteenth century, during the Hundred Years War. Belvès contains the remains of a castle, a fine old church, and some mellow-stone buildings, a good place to stop for the night.

From Belvès, the track climbs away steadily to the west, at no great height but never flat, and down into a narrow valley, south of Bouillac, which the path follows west to the village of Montferrand-du-Périgord, which has a medieval *château-fort,* some fine old houses, hotels and cafés, and makes a good place for lunch.

Head south from here, still through woods and copses, to a minor road and across another valley into St-Jean-de-Bannes. The country south from here is quite delightful, all open meadows lined by orchards, with the odd flock of sheep grazing in a field, wild flowers in plenty on the banks, and trees heavy with blossom or fruit in every orchard.

The path wanders gently through this countryside and the walker's pace will slow. Eventually the path crosses the *variante* which leads off to the *bastide* of Monpazier. Follow this *variante* to the south-east, into Monpazier for the next night stop, for Monpazier is a lovely little town, a gem of the *bastides*.

Next day, rejoin the main GR by taking the other arm of the *variante,* and follow it to link with the GR36 again at Maran, heading south across the D2 road, up a wooded valley and over open country to the mighty castle at Biron, which has to be visited, a task that will take an hour or more. From the ramparts of Biron the views are superb, and the village below the walls of this castle would fit on any picture postcard.

South of Biron lies the large village of Lacapelle-Biron, which has plenty of accom-

Above: **An informative waymark on the road to Cahors.**

modation, including a *gîte d'étape,* and could make a night stop. A number of GRs join at Lacapelle to make this a cross-roads of the GR trails, but our route on the next day lies to the east, a long, easy sweep for most of the morning, to the town of St-Front-sur-Lémance, at its confluence with the river Briolance.

St Front has a fortified church, a relic of the warring past, which was probably built by the Templars. The path crosses the river here, climbs the far hill to Bourdiel and arrives, after a long walk mostly through woods, at the crest of a steep-sided valley, and suddenly looks down at the towers of Bonaguil, a very fine medieval château which guards the frontier of the Lot. Bonaguil will keep any castle-lover occupied for a couple of hours, after which the path crosses the river there to climb through the woods and on to the village of St-Martin-le-Redon, on the Thèze, where the GR65, the Road to Compostela, comes in from the east

and departs, after a short conjunction, for the south.

The GR36 still heads eastwards however, on a path which overlooks the valley of the Lot to the south, on to the scattered town of Duravel, a very historic little spot, a little gem of *Querçois* architecture.

From here the path goes on eastwards across the spurs jutting out from the hills above the river, down to the Chapelle de Cazes, some way from the north bank, and so on to the next stop, the fair-sized riverside town of Puy-l'Evêque. Puy-l'Evêque is famous for the manufacture of porcelain, and the cultivation of grapes for the *vin de Cahors,* the delicious black wine of Quercy. There is plenty of accommodation, and so this is a good place to stay before moving out, close to the river now, to the little town of Prayssac.

The Lot is making immense sweeps through this part of Quercy, vast curves which add to its

Below left: Walkers about to cross the Dordogne river.

Below right: The Dordogne river has carved a path through the plateau country and so created this wide valley.

length and force walkers away into the northern hills to avoid walking long sections around the bends. From Prayssac the GR36 climbs to the plateau north of the steep cliff that reaches above the river and crosses this spur before descending steeply into Castelfranc, climbing up and out again for a yet longer walk across the high country before descending again, into the town of Luzech, which is well worth exploring, or stopping the night. The neck of land created by the winding Lot is so narrow here that Luzech is practically an island.

The path cross the Lot at Luzech, and curves round the south bank of the *cingle* or loop to St-Vincent-Rive-d'Olt, at the foot of a very steep hill, which the path circles before heading south back into empty country, and then east to the wine centre at Douelle.

From here, there is a last, long and marvellous walk across the high, practically empty country of the Lot, which brings the traveller over the hill and down into Cahors across the splendid fortified medieval bridge of Pont Valentré, a fitting end to this classic walk across the Dordogne and beyond.

Above left: **David Wickers enjoying a summer walk through maize fields.**

Below left: **The green and lovely Dordogne countryside close to Belvès.**

Above: **The spectacular castle at Montfort.**

107

Willow trees, streams and grazing cattle are all features of the Normandy landscape.

Distance: 174 miles (291km) and Val du Saire 21 miles (34km).
Time Required: Approximately two weeks.
Type of Walk: Moderate country, a mixture of farmland, gorse, heathland, fairly gentle going along clifftops and bays.
Season: Early spring to late autumn — even in winter if you wish.
Maps and Guide: FFPR-CNSGR *Topo-Guide GR223 Sentier Tour du Cotentin (Avranches to Barfleur). Michelin Green Guide : Normandy. Carte Verte* Nos. 6, 16 and 17.
Getting to the Start: By Townsend-Thoresen ferry to Cherbourg, then train to Avranches.

Introduction

This is an ideal walk for introducing British ramblers to the beauty and variety of the French countryside. There seems to be a curious phenomenon at work when the British choose a holiday destination in France. Those areas of the country nearest to Britain, with the exception of Brittany, receive far fewer visitors, other than 'passing trade', than many of those parts of the country that lie an extremely long and tiring journey away from the Channel ports.

This neglect of 'doorstep' France has nothing to do with the inferior beauty of its countryside or a shortage of Gallic atmosphere. True, the scenery of the north may lack the spectacular quality of, say, the Alps or Pyrénées or the drama of fiery rivers like the Tarn or the Ardèche, at points where they carve their paths through the great gorges; but despite the traditional British rush from the Channel coast en-route to somewhere else, Northern France has plenty to offer, especially if your main motive for holidaying is to get more than a suntan.

Once of the easiest-to-reach parts of pretty countryside can be found on the Cotentin peninsula, that stubby thumb of Normandy that pokes up into the Channel to the east of the Channel Isles. Reaching it couldn't be simpler (unless your memory of going there dates back to 1944 and the Allied Invasion). Today, most people arrive by way of those Townsend Thoresen ferries that ply regularly between Southampton and Cherbourg, a voyage which takes only a few hours.

The GR223 is by no means a wilderness trail. It follows paths either along the coast or just inland, passing through a score of small towns, villages or hamlets, and is ideal for those British walkers who want an easy-to-reach destination, with nothing remotely arduous by way of terrain, and the 'back-up' perks of *logis* and small hotels to break the route into short, easily-managed distances — and the restaurants! Normandy's food is delicious, especially if you like your fish served as straight from the sea as can be and don't mind risking an assault on the arteries from the heavy cream and butter sauces

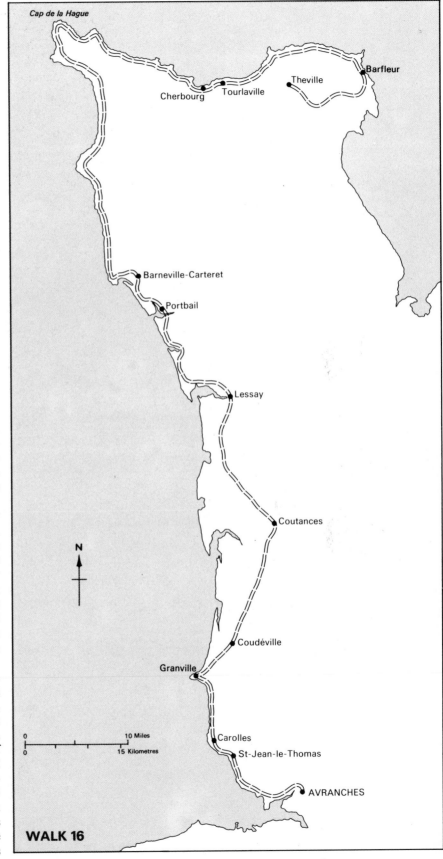

WALK 16

Mist shrouds the little fishing port of
Barneville-Carteret on the west coast
of the Cotentin.

which are the basis of Normandy cuisine.
Normandy is also apple country, which means
both fruit, *tartes aux pommes,* and the famous
cidre and Calvados brandy. Keep walking or
you will grow very fat!

The GR223 is, effectively, two routes. The
longer section begins at Urville, a few miles to
the west of Cherbourg, and accompanies the
Channel coastline as far as Avranches, although
having gone so far, who could resist continuing
along the GR22, around the estuary of the
Sélune and the Sée, to see the awesome bulk of

Mont-St-Michel out in the bay.

The shorter, eastern loop, the *Tour du Val de
Saire,* starts at Tourlaville and, from
Fermanville, begins a circuit that takes in the
port of Barfleur and the secretive little Val du
Saire. The GR223 is a walk which gives its main
allegiance to the sea, to sandy beaches often
backed by enormous dunes, with clifftop inter-
ludes and small fishing harbours, with plenty of
inland twists and turns, through low-lying
marshlands and gently curving scenery where
you will encounter tiny hamlets and ports at the

mouths of heavily silted estuaries.

Apart from the obvious geographical links with Britain, interpreted broadly to include an equally 'will-it, won't-it' climate with which to gamble, the Cotentin peninsula also shares close historic ties with England which span the two major conquests of 1066 and 1944, the first going north and the second south. Those who like gentle countryside and quiet, undiscovered places, will enjoy this classic walk.

The Route

Avranches, at the southern end of the Cotentin trail, sits about 300ft (100m) above the Sée-Sélune estuary and affords a number of excellent viewing spots to the bay of Mont-St-Michel, including the sight of the abbey itself, the best being from the interesting Botanic Gardens in the town centre. Avranches is one of the oldest towns in France, with plenty to distract the history buff from getting on with the miles ahead. There is, for example, a paving stone which stands on the site of the ancient

Top: **The western Cotentin south of the Nez de Joburg.**

Above: **Many of the apples grown in Normandy go to make their local liquor, Calvados.**

111

cathedral where, in 1172, the English King Henry II knelt to receive absolution from the Pope's legate for the murder of Thomas à Becket. A testimony to more recent times is the square named in honour of General Patton, whose headquarters stood here prior to the 1944 Allied breakthrough into Normandy.

The early stages of the trail adhere to the northern edge of the bay above the vast, flat, sand and marsh expanses, which look most breathtaking at sunset. The most spectacular sight, however, can be best seen from the peninsula Grouin du Sud, when the incoming tide arrives as a sheer wall, moving at a terrifying speed. It passes this peninsula at precisely one-and-a-quarter hours before High Tide, the times of which can be checked from the local newspaper. Appealing though it looks, don't be tempted to cross the sands to the abbey in a direct line. Such journeys are possible but risky without the company of a local guide who can be recruited from Gênets, the next village along the way.

In sharp contrast to the bay-side scenery, the path from St-Jean-le-Thomas follows along the top of cliffs, past Carolles, a smart seaside town with distinctly Edwardian airs, to Granville. This 'two-in-one' town has an old, granite stoned section with ramparts built by the English in the 1430s, as a rival stronghold to the fortifications of Mont-St-Michel, although three years after they were completed the English were driven out. The lower part of the town is both a commercial port and a tourist haven, with several hotels, restaurants, and a long beach.

Beyond the beach resort of Coudéville, the route turns inland, crosses the estuary of the Vanlée and the Sienne, with their timeless fishing ports, and crosses a productive countryside, a market garden corner of Normandy most famous for carrots which are ideally suited to the fast-draining, sandy soil hereabouts.

Coutances serves as the main religious centre of the Peninsula. Once an important Roman town, its magnificent Norman Gothic cathedral

Gathering shell fish close to Avranches.

stands on the same site as both a Roman temple and a fifth-century church, above the Bulsard valley. It miraculously escaped the bombing of 1944, even though the rest of the town was virtually razed to the ground.

After walking mostly along field paths, through very gently undulating scenery, you come to the forests of Pirou and, on the northern edge, a village with the remarkable name of Le Far West! Immediately beyond is a lonely, rather eerie desert, scrub and gorse-bush landscape with neither houses, trees nor livestock, known as the Landes de Lessay, or more colloquially, the 'Camargue of the North.'

Lessay itself is a port on the mouth of the river Ay, built around an outstanding twelfth-century Romanesque abbey church, founded by William the Conqueror's family, but the town is more famous today for its medieval Fair of the Holy Cross, still the most important fair in Normandy, held in the second week of September and one which draws an enormous number of horse, sheep and dog breeders and buyers, plus crowds of spectators who come to enjoy the music and merriment, plus the tasty roasts of lamb and geese.

After Lessay the GR223 follows the northern shore of the estuary and, at St Germain-sur-Ay, returns to the sea. Portbail is another historic town, set in the sand dunes, with the remains of a Roman baptistery. Barneville-Carteret is a popular French seaside resort where the footpath makes a delightful detour out around the Cap de Carteret. This is the nearest port to Jersey and therefore popular with both the fishing fleet and pleasure yachts during the summer. Here you follow in the old tracks of customs' officers patrolling the coast for smugglers, the *Sentiers des Douaniers*. Walking along the cliffs hereabouts, above some of the biggest sand dunes you are ever likely to see (some more than 300ft (90m) high), you should heed three warnings that are given in the *Topo-Guide:* look out for adders; be wary of strong winds; and don't try going down to walk on the beaches. Not only are the descents and ascents difficult but you may also find yourself cut off by the tide.

The northern section of the walk contains, conveniently so for short-stay visitors from across the waters, the most varied geography of the entire way. There are historic distractions too, such as the town of Vauville, an ancient place of pilgrimage, where waters, taken from the fountain of one 'Happy Thomas', are supposed to have amazingly rejuvenating effects; however, Thomas died in 1257. To the north lies the savage, steep and bay-indented coastline of the Cap de la Hague and the particularly awesome granite cliffs of the Nez de Jobourg which, at some 457ft (125m) are the highest cliffs in France, set above the treacherous waters known to yachtsmen as the Alderney Race.

At Goury, where the lighthouse is perched on a tiny offshore island, the trail turns sharply to the east. From the old fort of Omonville you can look across the bay to your destination, the busy port of Cherbourg. The designated path follows the coastline to Urville-Hague where you can catch a CTC bus to Cherbourg and the ferry home.

The start of the other segregated section of the trail, along the Val du Saire, begins at Tourlaville, south of Cherbourg. Before reaching the point of the Cap Levi on the Val du Saire walk, you pass the bay and the site of the ancient Roman port of Levi, which offered a rare place of shelter along this exposed northern coastline that lies between the lighthouse of Levi and the one at Gatteville. Gatteville lighthouse is one of the tallest in France and is open to the public. The currents off the shore are extremely dangerous to shipping and have claimed, among scores of other vessels, the famous *White Ship* carrying William, son of Henry I, and heir to the English throne.

Barfleur is everyone's favourite fishing port, especially to the hundreds of pleasure yachts that come here during the summer months. The town's star role in the history books is as one of the departure points for William the Conqueror's invasion of England on the date that is remembered by every British schoolchild. Barfleur served as the main port link to Britain for two centuries after. Today, the main attractions are the Hôtel du Phare, or the Hôtel des Fuchsias, perfect hotels for that end-of-the-walk celebration.

From Barfleur the path turns inland to follow the beautiful valley of the Saire before completing the circle at Théville, from where you can return to Cherbourg and catch the ferry home.

Walk 17 GR68 : A WALK IN THE SOUTHERN AUVERGNE

The river Tarn near Florac, at the beginning of the walk.

Introduction

We must confess a weakness for the hills of the Auvergne. They are high and long enough to be exciting and a challenge, yet they do not bar the path in the same forbidding manner as the high peaks of the Alps and Pyrénées. Other than in winter these hills are not difficult to cross, requiring only a certain skill with map and compass and the physical ability to keep going until the next village comes into sight. Besides, they are very beautiful, and unlike anything found in Britain, which is an inducement in itself. Mont Lozère, which gives a name to the *département,* is a splendid peak 5545ft (1690m) high, and effectively links the hills of the Massif Central with those of the Cévennes, two classic walking areas which this trail combines.

For all these reasons, which add up to a certain preference, a number of the walks in this book are centred on the Auvergne and the Cévennes. Personal preference apart, these are still classic walks, for they take the traveller through some superb walking country, into parts of France which few car-borne tourists ever enter.

This particular walk, the *Tour de Mont Lozère,* was a delightful find. I first used it to link up a section of the Robert Louis Stevenson Trail between Pont de Montvert and Florac, when we discovered that the traditional route alongside the Tarn had become a race-track road for heavy lorries, and a dangerous place for walkers.

The *Tour de Mont Lozère* is a splendid circular route, right round the high peak, very varied and by no means always hard, running through some of the prettiest places in the Tarn valley, such as Florac and Le Bleymard, with the chance to veer off at various points and climb up to the top of a mountain for views which, on a good clear day, might stretch to the shores of the distant Mediterranean.

Snows can lie late on the top of Mont Lozère, but this walk is perfectly possible from Easter until October, although it can be rainy and cold at night at either end of the season, and very hot indeed in high summer. Light boots or stout trainers are adequate and shorts are useful, although long trousers or breeches may save you from scratches in the scrub. Among the usual aids of suncream and lipsalve, a snake-bite kit might be useful.

There is adequate accommodation for those who wish to reduce their loads and use hotels, although booking ahead is advisable in high season. Those who wish to camp will have no trouble finding a pitch, but remember the high risk of fire in the woods, especially during July and August when the undergrowth is tinder-dry.

The Route

It is possible to pick up the GR68 at a number of points, with Florac as one popular starting point, but this description begins where the walk officially starts, in the little town of Villefort. This lies on the main railway line between Paris and Nîmes, to the east of the region. From Villefort the path follows the D66 out as far as the station, and then climbs up through the woods to the ruined hamlet of Montat, a huddle of tumbledown houses, then over the crest and into another, but still occupied hamlet, L'Habitarelle. From here, the path follows that of the GR44, across the river at Lieyros, up to Villespasses at 2770ft (845m), then across a brook, then another, up and down, hill following river valley into the village of Pomaret, a pleasant little place with a shop where it is possible to buy the ingredients for a picnic lunch by the river.

The ground is now rising quite steeply to the south, and the path climbs to the west, up to over 3280ft (1000m) at the Col de Bourbon, a splendid spot, then through a narrow gulley, and across several more brooks into the large village of Cubières, which has a hotel and could make a night stop, with 12 miles (20km) completed. It is, however, a very small hotel, and so it is best to skirt Cubières, contour the mountain on the track to Neyrac, past the little reservoir, on a very pleasant tree-lined route, shady on a hot

afternoon, and up to the Col Santel at 3920ft (1195m). Here the GR7 Draille du Gevaudan crosses the track, north to south, a useful checkpoint and one offering splendid views. It is possible to turn north now into Le Bleymard, where there is plenty of accommodation, and it only lies 1 mile (2km) north of the trail at this point. Le Bleymard is a pretty village, very typical of the area and worth visiting. Otherwise, descend into the Malavielle valley, over the stream and the D20 and along a wide forest trail into Orcières.

Those who did not stop at Le Bleymard, and are not camping, will still have a good distance to cover before they find shelter on the route, although there is plenty of accommodation off

The countryside levels out in the Southern Auvergne and gives good, firm, breezy walking.

Distance: 66 miles (110km).
Time Required: One or two weeks.
Type of Walk: A circular walk across the warm, varied hill-country of the Southern Auvergne.
Maps and Guides: FFPR-CNSGR: GR68 *Tour du Mont Lozère*. IGN *Carte Verte* No. 59. *Languedoc Roussillon,* by Neil Lands (Spur).
Getting to the Start: By train via Villefort to Paris-Nîmes.

WALK 17

Map showing GR68 circular route with locations including Bagnols-les-Bains, St Julien, Le Bleymard, Col des Sagnoles, Orcières, Col de Bourbon, Cubières, VILLEFORT, La Fage, Le Pont de Montvert, Tarn, L'Aubaret, Gourdouse, Les Bouzèdes, Pont-du-Tarn, Florac, Croix de Berthel.

the trail hereabouts, at St Julien or Bagnols-les-Bains. These last two places are reached by a *variante,* so no actual distance is lost. After Orcières the path follows a road west, out of the village up to a menhir, where the *variante* veers off to the right, and the main path climbs slightly and then descends steadily to the bottom of the Oultet brook in a well-marked track, then up again over the hill to meet a main road, the D41, running south from Bagnols. The path runs to the right of this road, up to the Col de la Loubière, 3875ft (1181m), past a *gîte d'étape,* which lies to the south of the trail at Auriac.

At the col there is a sudden sharp change of direction, for the path turns sharply right, or south, onto the Draille de la Margeride, another great drove road, which it follows up to another col, the Col des Sagnoles at 4445ft (1355m). The path climbs higher, keeping just east of the Serre des Countrasts at 4835ft (1475m), across a beautiful, open, windy tableland, then down, on a slightly longer but easier descent, to the Col or Croix des Faux at 4125ft (1258m). Here again, accommodation is limited to camping on the route, but there is a *gîte d'étape* one kilometre west of the Croix, at La Fage.

South of the Croix lies Rob's favourite kind

of country, which is open and rolling, at the 3000-ft (1000-m) mark with vast views, the odd scattered house or farm, perhaps a small village appearing on a hill from time to time, but essentially empty of people. This section of the path is fairly flat, but all the up and down work is worth it just to get up here into the 'great alone'. Walking up here can be difficult in times of mist or low cloud and, although the *draille* is marked with cairns, taking the occasional compass bearing can be useful.

Past Les Combrettes, the path starts to descend into that dramatic and spectacular natural wonder, the Gorges of the Tarn, which can be seen from the path at the 3760-ft (1233-m) mark, as it starts to descend in steep zig-zags, towards the Pont du Tarn at Florac, at around 1550ft (550m).

Florac is a pretty town, at the head of the highest section of the Tarn gorges. Here you will find the conjunction of a number of trails and it is a good place for a few days off, perhaps to take an excursion or a boat trip down the river.

The GR68 skirts through the northern outskirts of Florac and begins to climb again to the woods, through a mixture of orchards and chestnut groves, working round the south side of the mountain, over the ridge which runs north from the peak of La Chaumette, and then through thick forest, contouring steep slopes under some power lines to the Col de Sapet. Compass bearings can be a comfort here, but there is a road, if a minor one, the D20, which crosses this country, coming in from Le Pont de Montvert further north, so it is difficult to get very lost or to go far wrong. It is here that those who wish to avoid the heavy traffic on the Robert Louis Stevenson Trail, which is now the N598, can turn west on the GR68 for Florac.

From this checkpoint at Sapet, the GR68 sticks to the south side of the mountain for the Col de Planette, 3940ft (1292m), reached over a fairly testing up-and-down route. Accommodation hereabouts is in the solitary *gîte d'étape,* or several kilometres north of the route in the village of Le Pont de Montvert, reached on a minor road down the Martinet valley.

At the Col de Planette, the GR72 comes in from the north, another checkpoint, but our route climbs again, across the crest of the Massif de Bouges, with steep slopes to the south and marginally gentler slopes falling away to the north. Several attractive villages run up almost to the path which, as usual, is rising and falling and never flat, up to the Signal de Ventalon, from where it descends along the Draille du Languedoc on a long ridge falling to the north, to the Croix de Berthel at 3570ft (1088m), where there is shelter available in a *gîte* at nearby Auberge des Bastides.

This col at Ventalon is yet another Atlantic-Mediterranean water-shed, and a forest trail or *draille* leads down to the metalled road at L'Aubaret. L'Aubaret is well worth inspecting, an old fortified *bastide* village, set high in the mountains. The path follows the road east for a while to Pierres Froides, then over a stream, always winding but always bearing steadily to the east, round the crest of marvellous escarpments just east of Gourdouse, an abandoned hamlet. Follow the crest past Point 1396 into Les Bouzèdes.

From here it is a full day's walk of 15 miles (24km) to the north in order to complete the circuit at Villefort, but this can be extended a little if time allows by cutting off the trail at Les Bouzèdes, and dropping down a steep path into the large village of Génolhac. After a day's rest in Génolhac, a steep climb up a winding trail through the woods takes the traveller back to the path and the end of this journey by the railway station at Villefort.

A dry-stone-walled boundary path.

Walk 18 GR760: A WALK IN THE WINE COUNTRY

Introduction

A Beaujolais vineyard near Fleurie.

In a book of classic walks in France it seemed essential to include a walk through the wine country. The problem was, which one? France is richly endowed with vineyards, and most of them are set in beautiful, fairly rugged country; good wine comes from tough vines, grown in a certain adversity. It didn't take too long to settle on the Beaujolais, for while the wine itself is the best known of all French wines, the country itself is little-visited, and so remains archetypal France, unplagued by tourists. Indeed, Clochemerle, the one French village every Briton has heard of, is said to be based on the village of Vaux-en-Beaujolais, near Villefranche. They certainly have a warm welcome there, in the depths of the Caveau de Clochemerle.

The Beaujolais country has recently acquired its own GR trail, the GR760, *Sentier du Tour des Monts du Beaujolais,* which is made up by linking sections of the GRs 7, 76 and 7A to make the perfect route through this green and attractive region.

The Beaujolais country lies north and west of the great city of Lyon, a hilly region, studded with small villages, each one devoted to the cultivation of the vine. To the east lies the Rhône valley, to the west, the marching hills of the Forez. This walk actually crosses two modest hill ranges, the Monts du Lyonnais, which peak at the 3280-ft (1000-m) mark, and the slightly lower Monts du Beaujolais, which run up to 2625-2950ft (800-900m).

The walk is therefore at a fairly low altitude and although there is always snow on the tops in winter, this walk can be accomplished at any time of the year. It will appeal to all sorts of walker, for there are plenty of pitches for the backpacker, and enough accommodation in the villages to provide the long-distance walker with shelter every night. Except in high summer, the sort of equipment used for walking in Britain will be perfectly suitable, and in the hot months, shorts, hat and sun-cream are the only real essentials. The *Topo-Guide* recommends nine stages to complete the Tour, and the local *Syndicats* along the way are busy equipping these stages with *gîtes d'étape*.

The Route

It is possible to pick up the tour at several points as there are good connections from Lyon to all parts of the Beaujolais, but the description below follows the route laid out in the *Topo-Guide,* and begins in the town of L'Arbresle, a short distance north-west of Lyon.

The trail begins in the centre of the town, crosses the railway line and heads south, rising slowly to the village of Savigny, a pretty place with medieval houses, and a good place for a coffee stop after an hour on the trail. At Savigny the path skirts the walls of the old abbey to the Tresoncle brook and then heads west on minor roads to Lanay, where it picks up a footpath which contours the hillside at the 1640-ft (500-m) level to the ancient fortified farm at Bombeynon, and so to the Col du Mont d'Arjoux. Mont d'Arjoux itself at 2675ft (815m) lies a few score metres to the north, and it is worth walking up to the top of this little hill for fine views over the countryside.

This is gently rolling hill country which makes for very pleasant walking, through small woods, fields and vineyards, and there is another good viewpoint over all this from the calvary by the *gîte* at Montaly, at 2250ft (686m).

From here a narrow footpath leads down to Montrottier, which has hotels, bars and restaurants, and would be a good place for lunch. As you can see, this is a walk for the less committed walker who wants to enjoy the country and *all* it has to offer. Leave Montrottier by the road for St Martin and past the little Romanesque chapel to the Les Auberges cross-roads. This section of the walk is often along minor roads, and they lead into the town of Villechenève, a small, attractive town which would make a good night stop.

Leaving here, the path turns north, into the Bois d'Azole, skirting the hillside, and up a valley to the Tour Matagrin at 3280ft (1000m), and then down into the town of Violay after 5 miles (8km). After Violay, the countryside becomes a little wilder, the houses more scattered, the villages less frequent, and the path uses more footpaths and fewer small roads. The path follows the crest of the land at the 2625-ft (800-m) mark, from height to height, on a line marking one of these watersheds where the rivers to the west flow into the Atlantic, and those to the east into the Mediterranean. It also marks the dividing line between the *départements* of Loire and Rhône, and descends

Below: **A view of the Mont du Beaujolais.**

Bottom: **A shuttered shop front in a Beaujolais village.**

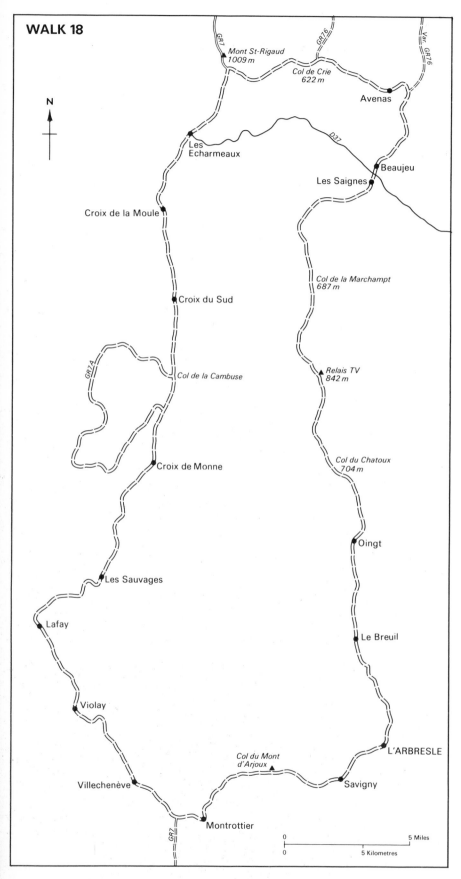

WALK 18

Mont St-Rigaud 1009 m
GR7
GR76
Var. GR76
Col de Crie 622 m
Avenas
Les Echarmeaux
D37
Beaujeu
Les Saignes
Croix de la Moule
Col de la Marchampt 687 m
GR7A
Croix du Sud
Col de la Cambuse
Relais TV 842 m
Col du Chatoux 704 m
Croix de Monne
Oingt
Les Sauvages
Le Breuil
Lafay
Violay
L'ARBRESLE
Col du Mont d'Arjoux
Savigny
Villechenève
GR7
Montrottier

0 ———— 5 Miles
0 ———— 5 Kilometres
N

Distance: 92 miles (154km).
Time Required: Two weeks.
Type of Walk: A gentle hill walk, over the vine-draped hills of the Beaujolais.
Maps and Guides: FFPR-CNSGR Guide No. 760, *Tour des Monts du Beaujolais. Burgundy*, Neil Lands (Spurbooks). IGN *Carte Verte* No. 43.
Getting to the Start: By train to L'Arbresle, via Lyon.

after 4 miles (6km) into the little hamlet of Lafay, before crossing more woodland, up to the road and track junction at the Col du Pin Bouchain at 2490ft (759m). From here the path descends, past the *gîte* at Crêt-Pivot, into the village of Les Sauvages.

The GR path runs north now, climbing rapidly, again picking a line along the west flank of the hill, with steep ridges to the right, and slightly gentler woodland to the left. The track is mostly through woodland, though good views appear on every hill and at the various cols which lead between them.

After the Croix de Monne, the path crosses the Col de la Croix des Fourches, 2545ft (776m), and climbs through the woods of Mollière, east of the 810m trig-point to the Croix des Aliziers. Here the only major *variante* on the journey, the GR7A, runs off to the left. This is a circular route of 16 miles (26km), which rejoins the main trail only 4 miles (6km) north of Aliziers, at the Col de la Cambuse 2320ft (707m).

Our main route lies to the north-east, past the Roche de Fées, a good landmark, through the great forest of Ramenoux. Still on the crest of the hills, moving from high point to high point, make for the Croix du Sud, and then, leaving the village of St Bonnet-le-Troncy to the west, or stopping there for the night or a meal, move on along the ridges, the woods falling away to the east, the land rising and more open away to the west. This countryside is very varied, a mixture of pasture, arable land, vineyards and orchards, with the Monts du Beaujolais looming up on the right. The path crosses the D-54 at the Col de Farardy at 2810ft (856m), and after the Croix de la Moule at 2950ft (900m) starts to descend, skirting the Bois de Lafay, into the little town of Les Echarmeaux. This town is well worth a stop and has a *gîte d'étape,* several hotels and a number of good restaurants. After a stop, or even a day off here, the path picks up the crest again to the Roche d'Ajoux at 3090ft (970m), the Croix d'Ajoux at 2805ft (855m), and on to the Col de Patoux at 3000ft (915m). A little north of here the path turns sharply south-east, passing through a col between two peaks, Mont Monet at 3285ft (1001m) and Mont-St-Rigaud at 3310ft (1009m). Both are worth ascending.

East of Mont-St-Rigaud the countryside descends, the path crossing a land empty of people around Mont Chonay at 2490ft (760m), and down to the road junction at the Col de Crie at 2040ft (622m), where the GR76 sweeps in from the north. These two paths combine here and head east to the village of Le Pardon, past a Romanesque church into Avenas. Avenas lies in fairly open country, with a higher ridge to the south, the Mont de Rochefort. Our path skirts this height to the east, winding through the vineyards into the town of Beaujeu, which is one of the great wine centres of the Beaujolais. If you have space and weight to spare, put a bottle or two in your pack, noting that the local people like their red wine chilled.

It is vineyards all the way now, through Les Saignes, climbing south up to the Casse-Froide col, keeping east of Mont Soubran at 2930ft (894m), to the Col de la Marchampt at 2255ft (687m). We are, as always on this walk, still moving along ridges close to the various small peaks, first to the small hill past la Croix-Desplaces and then up to the TV masts which top the peak at 2760ft (842m). Three miles (5km) to the south, and a worthwhile diversion off this trail, lies the village of Vaux-en-Beaujolais, better known to us Francophiles as Clochemerle.

The main path goes on through pine woods, crosses the main N504 road, and into the hamlet of St Cyr-le-Chatoux, small but still attractive, and then up again through the woods to the Col du Chatoux at 2310ft (704m), and on to the very attractive little town of Oingt, a well-preserved relic of the Middle Ages and well worth a visit or even a night stop in the *gîte*.

South of Oingt, the countryside becomes even more populated, with many small farms and houses dotted about among the vineyards. The next town, Le Bois d'Oingt, is quite large, and the route out follows the road to Legny, and on to Le Breuil. After Le Breuil, the end is almost in sight, with the path picking a short way south into L'Arbresle and the end of this journey.

Top: **The height of the *vendange*, the annual grape picking.**

Middle: **A footpath through the vineyards.**

Bottom: **Walking in the surrounding forests above the vineyards of Beaujolais.**

Walkers heading south from Mont-St-Michel.

Introduction

Before setting out across the Pyrénées, on the final walk of this book, it occurred to us that a number of British walkers might still feel reluctant to leave their well-remembered native hills for any foreign walk, however classic. Before we finish, should we not provide an introduction, and lead our readers into France on an easy but interesting trail? Fortunately we had a suitable walk available, close to the port of St Malo, and finishing at the splendid island fortress of Mont St Michel. This walk deserves to be included here because it was the first of the now classic current series of walks which Brittany Ferries organise for the travel writers, as a way of introducing them to the delights of France away from the tourist track. If it works for the travel writers, why not for the average walker?

This trail begins outside Rennes and can be easily completed in four days. Those who want more walking can turn west after Mont-St-Michel and return to St Malo along the coast through Cancale, which will take a further two days. The terrain is easy, but it can be muddy, so light boots and gaiters are advisable. There is plenty of accommodation, wild camping is possible, and there is a small *gîte d'étape* at La Lande Ragot. This is the perfect end-of-season walk for the soft days of autumn.

The Route

Leave the centre of Rennes along the Canal d' Ille et Rance, heading for the lock of L'Ecluse Robinson at St Grégoire. Follow the towpath from here, a well-drained level way to Betton, 5 miles (8km), which will make a good coffee stop and where the path crosses the railway line, still heading north, but bearing a little east for La Petite Hublais, and into the vast forest of Rennes. Forest rides seam their way through the trees and it is quite easy to get lost, but the path eventually reaches the lake or *étang des* Maffrais, and skirting Liffré, which has plenty of good hotels and restaurants, arrives at the *gîte d'étape* at La Lande Ragot, on a small farm set about with apple orchards.

From here the footpath arrows north through Ercé, and out on a minor road to Bon-Air, and so into the Forêt de la Haute-Sève. Cross this to the east to the D23 junction at the Carrefour de la Grande-Breche, then north to La Croix Bagot and on to the river Couesnon. This river marks the boundary between Brittany and Normandy.

Follow this river north towards the Moulin de Guyon, past Mézières, (which would make a good second night stop), and head on to Antrain. This third day, from Mézières to

Antrain, is the most rugged section of a never-difficult walk. The path leaves the river after Guyon, and cuts due north, down the Chemin des Anglais, past Ste Apolline, through Romazy, a good place for lunch, or another night stop, and then on, up the east bank of the Couesnon to Antrain. Antrain has plenty of

Walkers enjoying the dappled shade in the Forêt de Rennes.

Distance: 60 miles (100km).

Time: One week.

Type of Walk: A gentle walk across the woods and farming country of Brittany.

Maps and Guides: FFRP-CNSGR Guide GR39. *Sentier Manche-Océan* (Rennes to Mont-St-Michel). *Brittany & The Bretons* by Keith Spence (Gollancz). *A Visitor's Guide to Brittany*, Neil Lands (Moorland Publishing Co.). *Brittany (Michelin Green Guide)*. IGN *Carte Verte* No. 16.

Getting to the Start: By Brittany Ferry to St Malo and then by train to Rennes.

WALK 19 — MONT-ST-MICHEL

Top right: **The muddy paths of the GR39 require stout footwear.**

Bottom right: **Mont-St-Michel is dramatically flood-lit by night.**

accommodation, including a *gîte d'étape,* and is quite a large town.

Leaving Antrain for the north, the path enters another forest and climbs steadily to a low crest at Vieux-Viel and it is from here that the walker will get that first view of Mont-St-Michel peaking the skyline to the north. After this encouraging sight, the path descends into Pleine Fougères and after a few more miles into Pontorson. Pontorson is the main centre for

travellers visiting Mont-St-Michel, and a good place to stop before walking out through streets draped with the flags of Brittany and Normandy, past the racecourse and along the dyke beside the Couesnon, to the island-abbey of Mont-St-Michel. The Bretons will tell you that the Couesnon is to blame for the fact that this splendid island now belongs to Normandy. The Couesnon, which marks the frontier, once flowed round the eastern side of the island, but after a storm the stream changed to send the river round the western walls, which thus transferred ownership of the island to Normandy.

A half-day exploring Mont-St-Michel ends the main part of this journey, but if you have time to spare, walk west along the road through Cancale and end where you arrived in France, at the corsair city of St Malo.

Walk 20 A MOUNTAIN WALK IN THE PYRENEES

Introduction

This footpath, the GR10 *Sentier des Pyrénées,* is one of the world's great walks, and merits inclusion here as a Classic Walk of France. It is also one of the longest walks in France, a 480-mile (700-km) walk across the high spine of the Pyrénées, from the Atlantic to the Mediterranean. To complete the full distance would take a fit walker six or seven weeks, and since the walks in this book are designed to fit into the free time available to ordinary folk, we had to select an area which would offer an example of what the total walk could offer, and yet be a good, complete walk in its own right. A great deal of humming and ha-ing then followed before we came down on that section of the walk that lies between Larrau in the Basque country and runs across the *comté* of Béarn, to finish in the green valleys of Bigorre. This is a high mountain walk which runs up to the Franco-Spanish fronter at La-Pierre-St-Martin, crosses many high cols, and even provides the opportunity for those who have a little extra time on their hands to take the *variante* around the Pic du Midi d'Ossau, one of the great peaks of the Pyrénées.

The greatest attraction of this splendid walk lies in the marvellous Pyrénées themselves, a wonderful range of mountains which are still, at least when compared with the Alps, virtually unknown to British walkers. They run for 250miles (400km) across that neck of land which separates France from Spain, reaching their peak at 11,165ft (3404m) at the Pico de Aneto, which actually lies on the Spanish side of the frontier. The Pyrénées is not a continuous chain, for there is a gap, the Val d'Aran, east of Bigorre, through which the river Garonne, here called the Spanish Garona, runs over into France. It is also worth noting that these north-facing French slopes are far steeper than those on the Spanish side, where the Pyrénées run softly out into Spain.

Since these French slopes are both high and north-facing, one must beware of the elements. Snow will lie here throughout the year, and the high cols may not be open until mid-June. I have seen the Col du Tourmalet blocked as late as July. The snow lies again from mid-October, and inevitably, the hills are as busy as they ever get between mid-July and the end of August. British walkers should aim to travel at any time from the last week of June until the third week of October, but remembering to camp or book well ahead if they aim to walk in high season.

Distance: 77 miles (125km).
Time Required: Two weeks.
Type of Walk: A high mountain walk for fit, experienced hill-walkers and well-equipped backpackers.
Maps and Guides: FFPR-CNSGR *Sentier des Pyrénées (Tronçon du Béarn).* IGN 1:50,000 for Larrau, Laruns, Argelès-Gazost. *The French Pyrénées,* Neil Lands (Spurbooks). *Pyrénées West,* Arthur Battagel, (West Col).
Getting to the Start: By train and bus via Pau to Larrau.

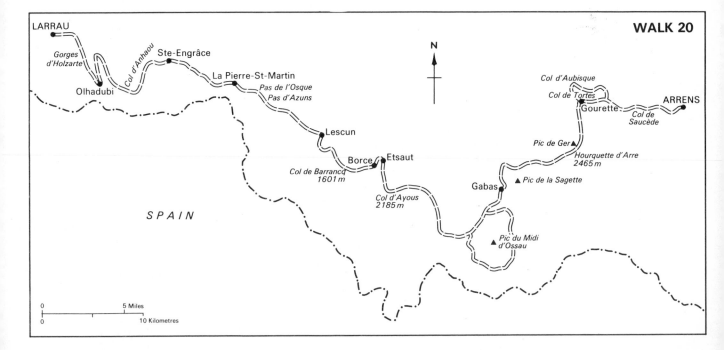

The Randonnées Pyrénéennes organisation in St Girons, is well worth contacting by any walker contemplating a trip in the Pyrénées. Please also note that we recommend 1:50,000 scale IGN maps for the walk rather than the 1:100,000 scale which is adequate in less rugged areas.

In high season, the *abris* and the CAF huts will certainly be crowded, and although no walker is ever turned away, those who intend to stay high should backpack, making periodic descents into the valley for a day off or to see a little of the land below. Full lightweight camping gear will be necessary, and the equipment should include windproofs, shorts, a hat and suncream. An ice-axe should certainly be carried at either end of the season, if not at all times.

The CNSGR *Topo-Guide* allows seven days for this route, but we recommend taking at least ten, allowing a full fourteen days for the holiday. This will give the walker time to scramble up the odd peak, spend a day camping by a mountain lake, or simply relaxing. This is a hill walk, not a race.

The Route

The walk begins in the Basque village of Larrau, and first runs almost due east towards Logibaria, and then south to skirt the deep divided gorges of the Holzarte. This part of the walk is not particularly high at about 2790ft (850m), and follows a minor road for much of the way, until it crosses the gorge to the south side of the eastern arm where the path begins to climb in zig-zags through the woods up to Olhadubi, at 2755ft (840m), at the head of the eastern arm. These Basque names are tongue-twisters and since the local *patois* is even worse, be careful with the map-reading; you may be able to ask the way, but will you be able to understand the reply? A bridge crosses the torrent at Olhadubi and the path turns north, contouring to the Point Côte, at 2805ft (855m), where the first real climb begins. This is attractive rocky country, with ridges jutting up in all directions, and the path climbs and climbs (and climbs), to the limit of the Larrau commune at the Col d'Anhaou at 4540ft (1383m).

Opposite page, top: **Snow still lies on the Col du Tourmalet even in midsummer.**

Opposite page, bottom: **The Pyrénées are full of beautiful lakes including this one at Néouvielle.**

Above left: **Good map reading is essential in the wild, desolate countryside of the Pyrénées.**

Top: **The Pic du Midi d' Ossau. This spectacular crag is not improved by the radar and TV station at the top.**

Above: **Even in summer an ice axe should be carried in the Hautes Pyrénées.**

The Pyrénées around Gourette.

who have already spent one night in the hills may wish to press on to Ste-Engrâce, a short distance away, which has an hotel, a couple of restaurants, various *gîtes* and other leisure possibilities. It's a very Basque village, well worth a stop for lunch or the night, and usually full of weary walkers in summer.

Pick up the footpath signs again by the church and turn east towards the stream, then around the mountain to Ferme Zolan and up to the edge of another gorge, Ibarra, at 2380ft (725m). This marks the end of the Basque country for the gorge divides the Basque region of the Soule from the French Comté of Béarn. The path crosses the north end of the gorge and starts a steep zig-zag climb through the woods, heading first south-east and then due south to the Cabane de Coup at 4990ft (1522m). This is an open spot, with good views over the mountains of the eastern Basque country, and the path climbs on to plateau and to the Col de la Pierre-St-Martin, which also marks the frontier with Spain. The local farmers and shepherds from both sides of the frontier share the mountain pastures hereabouts and meet on the col each year on the 13th July to sort out their flocks, have a party, and celebrate centuries of shared experience. From the col the path descends gently to the ski resort of Arette-la-Pierre-St-Martin, which looks much better if seen in winter, when snow hides the signs of high-rise construction. It consists of concrete apartment blocks, but there is at least plenty of accommodation, and the resort, like most Pyrénéan ski centres, is also trying hard to cater for those summer visitors who enjoy the mountains. You may not like it, but the views are superb.

Follow the road out, down the mountain, for a kilometre or so, and then head east on a footpath which climbs east to the Col de Mahourat. There are ski lifts everywhere, but these soon get left behind as the path reaches the plateau at Camlong, climbs steadily to the ridge ahead, at 6305ft (1922m) and drops down the far side of this re-entrant and so south to the Pas d'Azuns at 6145ft (1873m). From up here there is a marvellous wild panorama of the Oloron valley and, beyond, to the Pic d'Anie at 8215ft (2504m).

The path descends from the col and turns east, under the Orgues de Camplong, a high rock wall which looms to the north, past the *refuge* at Laberouat, and down the hillside to the resort at Lescun at 2950ft (900m). This section of the walk, with views to the high peaks of the Pyrénées and the valleys of the Aspe and Oloron, is the most striking of the entire route and a memorable section of the GR10.

From here the path descends, through some open pasture dotted with barns used for the *transhumance* or bi-annual flock and herd movements, to the *Sentier de Kakouéta*, a footpath which overlooks the deep and spectacular gorges of the *Kakouéta*, one of the great natural wonders of the Western Pyrénées. The path descends steeply to the river, or *gave de Kakouéta*, at 3120ft (952m), where there is a ford and climbs again, very steeply, to the Cayolar de Larregorry, at 4025ft (1227m). Then we follow a ridge, descending slightly with great views down on the Gorge, to Pont sur l'Heylet. For the record, the Basque name for this spot is *Erreguignaneko Zubia*, which will give the walker some idea of the complexities of the Basque tongue. In any language, it's a pretty spot and a good place to camp, although those

Lescun is a little place, popular with walkers and climbers, with one good hotel and several restaurants. It would be enjoyable to rest up here for a day or two and walk, lightly laden, to the Lac de Lhurs in the next valley, or up to some of the more accessible local peaks. These need be no more than scrambles, but they make for enjoyable day-walks.

Leaving Lescun, head south, climbing to the east after a while, for the ridge above Lhurs, continuing across to the stream at Labadie, a good camping spot. From here it is a short walk to Lhurs and to commence the steep climb to the Col de Barrancq at 5250ft (1601m). This spot, although high, is heavily forested, but there is a path to the right along the ridge which leads out of the trees and offers splendid views of the next high point on the walk, the rearing snow-tipped Pic du Midi d'Ossau.

The path drops steeply from here to the mountain village of Borce at 2130ft (650m), a three-hour descent which loses a thousand metres in height down to the banks of the Gave d'Aspe. Borce has a shop and plenty of bed and breakfast accommodation (chambre d'hôte). A short walk leads to Etsaut, which although smaller, has an hotel. Etsaut is also one of the places for entering the Pyrenean National Park, and so popular with walkers which the railway brings up here by the score.

Go south from Etsaut, keeping beside the road, towards the Fort du Portalet, and east along the Chemin de la Mature. Note the relic, even here, of the days of sail. These tall, straight trees of the Pyrénées made excellent masts, and they were felled and manhandled down this path to rig the shipping in the Biscay ports. The path mounts to an open plateau, skirting the gorge, and so up to the cabin at Baigt de St Cours, 5120ft (1560m), which marks the western limit of the vast *Parc National des Pyrénées Occidentales,* one of the great French National Parks, a paradise for wildlife.

The path now starts to climb across several cols, to the Col de Larry at 6990ft (2130m) and the Col d'Ayous at 7170ft (2185m). From here it is an easy half-hour's scramble to the Pic d'Ayous at 7505ft (2288m) which lies just along the ridge to the north-east.

Returning to the Col d'Ayous, descend to the lake at Roumassot, and down again to the Lac de Bious-Artigues at 4650ft (1417m), the starting point for the one major *variante* on this journey, the *Tour du Pic du Midi d'Ossau*. It will take a full day to encircle this great mountain, so those who attempt it — and all should — will need to leave early and walk steadily, returning to the Lac de Bious-Artigues, which is actually a reservoir, in the late evening.

A view of the Hautes Pyrénées from a valley near Pau.

After leaving the lake, the next notable spot is Gabas, a mountain village with several hotels, from where the path veers north to the west of the Pic de la Sagette, and turns east, on a fairly level though never smooth route, to the Carrefour de Piet and the Corniche des Athas, with the Pic de Ger a fine sight just to the north of the path.

The Cabanes de Cézy, set in an open alpine pastureland at 5350ft (1630m), is a good camping spot, and from here the path climbs again, to Hourquette d'Arre at 8085ft (2465m), then down to the Lac d'Anglas and another ski resort, Gourette. Like La Pierre-St-Martin to the west, Gourette is a modern resort and looks at its best in winter. It is, however, a good walking centre, with shops, hotels, plenty of accommodation, and the more marvellous countryside is set round about. From Gourette the path climbs to the east to the Col de Tortes, then follows the RN618 road to the Col d'Aubisque. This is one of the most spectacular mountain roads in France, and well worth following, set as it is high in the mountains, sweeping across open grassy country, a splendid windswept walk between the peaks to the Col de Saucède. From here the path descends steeply at last to Arrons and the end of this journey ... unless you have the time and the energy to walk on and on across the Pyrénées to sink your feet at last into the cool blue waters of the Mediterranean, still many hard miles away.

NATIONAL AND REGIONAL PARKS

La Fédération des Parcs Naturels
4 rue de Stockholm
75008 Paris
France
Tel: 294 90 84

Parc National des Cévennes
Chateau de Florac
BP4 - 48400 Florac
France
Tel: (66) 45-01-75

Parc National des Ecrins
7 rue du Colonel Roux
Boite Postale 142
05004 GAP Cédex
France
Tel: (92) 51-40-71

Parc National du Mercantour
13 rue Maccarani
06000 Nice
France
Tel: (93) 87-86-10

Parc National des Pyrénées Occidentales
Route de Pau – B.P. 300
65013 Tarbes
France
Tel: (62) 93 30 60

Parc National de Port Cros
50 avenue Gambetta
83400 Hyères
France
Tel: (94) 65-32-98

Parc National de la Vanoise
135 rue du Docteur Juliand
BP 105
73003 Chambéry
France
Tel: (79) 62-30-54

Regional Parks

Parc Naturel Régional d'Armorique
Menez-Meur
29247 Hanvec
France
Tel: (98) 68 81 71

Parc Naturel Régional de Brière
180 Ile de Fédrun
44720 Saint Joachim
France
Tel: (40) 88 42 72 et 39

Parc Natural Régional de Brotonne
2 Rond Point Marbec
76580 Le Trait
France
Tel: (35) 91 83 16

Parc Naturel Régional de Camargue
Le Mas du Pont de Rousty
13200 Arles
France
Tel: (90) 97 10 93

Parc Naturel Régional de la Corse
B.P. 417
20184 Ajaccio Cedex
France
Tel: (95) 21 56 54

Parc Naturel Régional de la Foret d'Orient
Maison du Parc
10220 Piney
France

Parc Naturel Régional du Haut Languedoc
B.P. No 9
34220 Saint Pons
France
Tel: (67) 97 02 10

Parc Naturel Régional des Landes de Gascogne
Préfecture
29 rue Victor Hugo
40011 Mont de Marsan
France
Tel: (58) 75 84 40

Parc Naturel Régional de Lorraine
Centre Culturel des Prémontrés
B.P. 35
54700 Pont à Mousson
France
Tel: (83) 81 11 91

Parc Naturel Régional du Lubéron
Avenue des Druides
84400 APT
France
Tel: (90) 74 08 55

Part Naturel Régional du Marais Poitevin
Val de Sèvre et Vendée
19 rue Bujault
79000 Niort
France
Tel: (49) 28 38 79

Part Naturel Régional de la Montagne de Reims
86 rue Belin
51100 Reims
France
Tel: (26) 40 43 84

Part Naturel Régional du Morvan
Maison du Parc
Saint Brisson
58230 Mont Sauche
France
Tel: (86) 78 70 16

Part Naturel Régional Normandie Maine
Le Chapitre
61320 Carrouges
France
Tel: (33) 27 21 15

Parc Naturel Régional du Pilat
Le Moulin de Virieu
2 rue Benay
42410 Pelussin
France
Tel: (74) 59 65 24

Parc Naturel Régional du Queyras
Avenue de la Gare
B.P. No 3
05600 Guillestre
France
Tel: (92) 45 06 23

Parc National Régional de Saint Amandraismes
"Le Luron"
357 rue Notre Dame D'Amour
59230 Saint Amand Les Eaux
France
Tel: (27) 48 78 77

Parc Naturel Régional du Vercors
Chemin des Fusillés
B.P. 14
38250 Lans en Vercors
France
Tel: (76) 95 40 33

Parc Naturel Régional des Volcans d'Auvergne
Château de Montlosier
Randanne
63210 Rochefort Montagne
France
Tel: (73) 21 27 19

Parc Natural Régional des Vosges du Nord
la Petite Pierre
67290 Wingen sur Moder
France
Tel: (88) 70 46 55

In Preparation

Mission d'Etude pour un parc naturel régional de Picardie Maritime
Préfecture
B.P. 1600
53 route de la République
80009 Amiens Cedex
France
Tel: (22) 92 16 78

Mission d'Etude pour un parc naturel régional de la Haute Vallée de Chevreuse
Préfecture 2 place Louis Barthou
78010 Versailles Cedex
France
Tel: 951 82 00 Poste 20 68

Mission d'Etude pour un parc national régional du Jura Gessien
Sous Préfecture
01170 GEX
France
Tel: (50) 41 50 29 (mairie)

Mission d'Etude pour les parcs naturels régionaux de l'Audomarois Monts de Flandre et du Boulonnais
Espace naturel régional
Région Nord pas de Calais
185-187 Bd de la Liberté
59800 Lille
France
Tel: (20) 30 82 81

Fédération des parcs naturels de France
4 rue de Stockholm
75008 Paris
France
Tel: 294 90 84

USEFUL ADDRESSES

Maps

MacCarta Ltd
122 Kings Cross Road
London WC1X 9DS
Tel: (01) 278 8278

Stanfords Map Centre
Long Acre
London WC2
Tel: (01) 836 1321

IGN Map Centre
Rue la Boetie
75008 Paris
France

Information

The French Government Tourist Office (FGTO)
178 Piccadilly
London W1V 0AL
Tel: (01) 491 7622

French Rail (SNCF)
178 Piccadilly
London W1V 0AL
Tel: (01) 493 4451/2

Club Alpin Francais (CAF)
7 rue la Boetie
75008 Paris
France

Austrian Alpine Club
(CAF-UK Affiliate)
Longcroft House
Fretherne Road
Welwyn Garden City
Herts AL8 6QP
Tel: (07073) 31133

The Confraternity of St James
(GR65)
57 Leopold Road
London N2
Tel: (01) 883 4893

**Fédération Française de la Randonnée Pédestre
(FFRP-CNSGR)**
8 avenue Marceau
75008 Paris
France

CIMES-GTA (for the Alps)
Maison du Tourisme
BP227-38019 Grenoble Cedex
France
Tel: (76) 54-34-36

CIMES Pyrénées (for the Pyrénées & Basque
Country)
3 square Balague
09200 Saint-Girons
France
Tel: (61) 66-40-10

CORAMIP (for the Midi-Pyrénées and the
Pyrénées chain)
12 rue Salambo
31200 Toulouse
France
Tel: (61) 47-11-12

ATR (for Languedoc-Roussillon)
12 rue Roch
34000 Montpellier
France
Tel: (67) 66-24-19

CHAMINA (for the Massif Central)
5 rue Pierre-Le-Vénérable
63000 Clermont-Ferrand
France
Tel: (73) 92-82-60

GTJ (for the Jura)
1 place de la 1ère-Armee-Francaise
25041 Besançon Cedex
France
Tel: (81) 80-92-55

ABRI (for Brittany)
3 rue des Portes-Mordelaises
35000 Rennes
France
Tel: (99) 79-36-26

Agriff (for the Ile de France)
64 rue de Gergovie
75014 Paris
France
Tel: 545-31-02

AGEP (for Picardie)
BP 0342
80003 Amiens Cedex
France
Tel: (22) 92-64-64

ADRI (for Alpes de Haute Provence)
14 boulevard Victor-Hugo
04000 Digne
France
Tel: (92) 31-37-70

ADDTP (for the Côte d'Azur)
3 impasse Baudin
83000 Toulon
France

ADDRAM-CRDP (for the Alpes-Maritimes)
Villa Taema
Montaleigne
067000 Saint-Laurent-du-Var
France
Tel: (93) 31-76-64

BIBLIOGRAPHY

Walking in France, Rob Hunter, (Oxford Illustrated Press or Hamlyn Paperbacks).

Travels with a Donkey in the Cévennes, Robert Louis Stevenson, (Folio Society).

Walking in the Alps, Brian Spencer, (Moorland Publishing).

100 Hikes in the Alps, Ira Spring & Harvey Edwards, (The Mountaineers).

The Road to Santiago, Walter Starkie, (John Murray).

Guide des Logis et Auberges de France, (FGTO – Annual).

National Parks of Western Europe, Angus Waycott, (Vango).

Pyrénées West, Arthur Battagel, (West Col).

Pyrénées Centre, Arthur Battagel, (West Col).

Winter Skills, Rob Hunter, (Constable,

The Outdoor Companion, Rob Hunter, (Constable).

Britain at Your Feet, Art Pederson & David Wickers, (Hamlyn).

Guide du Randonneur, G. H. Viaux (FFPR-CNSGR)

Haute Randonnée Pyrénéenne, G. Vernon, (CAF).

Expeditions, Blashford-Snell & Ballentine, (Faber)

Guide, Camping-Caravanning, (Touring Club de France – Annual).

INDEX